Cornell Effect

A Family's Journey toward
Happiness, Fulfillment and Peace

Lauren,
Love Your Life!! JW

cornell cranham
Kim Cranham

JOHN C. CRANHAM DDS

Distribution by Bublish, Inc.

ISBN: 978-1-64704-265-3 (Hardback)
ISBN: 978-1-64704-264-6 (Paperback)
ISBN: 978-1-64704-263-9 (eBook)

THIS BOOK IS DEDICATED TO:

Children's Hospital of the Kings Daughters (CHKD) and **Team Cornell**—the many doctors, nurses, and therapists who saved our son's life, most notably: Nurse Shirley; Nurse Elise; While we will not use the actually names of the Doctors in this book, you know who you are, and we are forever in your debt.

Our many friends and coworkers who have been with us on this journey: the Bowen family; the Ozmon family; the Wood family; the Jacques family; the Angelelli family; the faculty and staff of The Dawson Academy, especially Joan Forrest, Lenny Hess, Drew and Ellen Cobb, and Glenn and Janet Dupont; and the past and present members of my dental practice, Kim Richardson, Brandi Dezzani, Holly Rice, Mariah Scofield, Sarah Alexander, Kristen Cox, Kelly Brown, Presley Peele, and Krissie Markham. Many of you supported us during the darkest times and were there to celebrate the great times.

Dr. Pete E. Dawson, my mentor and friend, who first put the idea into my head of getting our story down on paper. He was one of the most productive, caring, and disciplined people I have ever met, and he was relentless in his encouragement of completing this project. While he is not here to see the final product, he lived through many of the stories with me. I miss him dearly.

Our extended family, who supported us the whole way: the Kelley Clan, Mag, Lynn, David, Sarah, Brian, Amy, Catharine, Emme, Campbell, Patrick, and Addy; the Cranham Clan, Barb, Karen, and Scott; and the Davidson Clan, Flip, Kay, Rob, Kathy, Tim, Sue, Chris, Abby, Matt, Stephanie, Barrett, Cassidy, Blake, Alisha, Ryan, and Jessica. While we could feel your concern, none of you blinked when we brought Cornell home with us. Your support meant and means more than you will ever know.

Kaitlyn and Kristen, who had the best seats in the house. Kim and I know this decision did not always make your life easy, something we spent countless hours worrying and praying about. But how you view the world now is inspiring. I am so proud of the women you have become. Your mom and I love being your parents.

Cornell, who inspired this book. You overcame more obstacles by the age of three than most of us will face in our entire lives. Your ability to forgive and to handle your challenges with grace, joy, and peace is something that I will never completely understand but will forever strive to emulate. People say that Kim and I were put on this earth to save you. I have come to believe it was the other way around. Being your daddy has been one of the great joys of my life.

Kim, my wife, my best friend, and the rock of our family. You were the first to catch Cornell's vision, and you had the courage to dig in your heels and fight for him. Quite simply, you are the best person I know. I am so blessed to get to share my life with you. Thanks for starting this incredible journey.

God, the true author of this story. Thank you for putting Cornell in our lives, for allowing us to love and learn from him, and for giving me the skill set to share this story.

CONTENTS

FOREWORD

The way I remember it, he was wearing sandals and a Hawaiian shirt while chomping on a Swedish meatball and grazing the appetizers. I was at a cocktail party following a lecture by the world's most renowned dentist. Knowing no one in the room, I struck up a conversation with John Cranham because he was the most casual person among a crowd full of sport coats and pantsuits.

I was a more than a little surprised the next morning when John, my new buddy, now dapper in a coat and tie, was introduced by the revered Dr. Peter Dawson as the day's speaker. The previous day, Dr. Dawson had set off light bulbs in the heads of hundreds of dentists from around the world. That day, Dr. John Cranham completed the circuit by connecting with his audience on a level that few teachers achieve.

Over the next few years, John became my mentor. On a regular basis, I would squeeze my six-foot, six-inch, 320-pound frame into a small Cessna and fly from Pennsylvania to Chesapeake, Virginia, to spend time with John at his office. My time with John inspired me to become not only a better dentist, but a better husband and father. He helped chart a course for me to use dentistry to create a family-centered lifestyle and a new kind of dental health system for my community.

When I spend time with John, I don't just study dentistry. I study how he teaches and how he galvanizes people to find passion and purpose in their lives. The secret is his sincere and persistent pursuit of possibilities. But John Cranham did not develop this fortitude on his own. Much of it was learned by observing his son, Cornell's, insatiable appetite for life, as he overcame incredible odds. John has told this story from the podium too many times to count and has inspired literally thousands of people to be better. This is "the Cornell Effect."

—Mike Verber, DMD

PROLOGUE

On February 2, 1994, my wife, Kim, and I went to the hospital to pick up our boy. But it wasn't the kind of thing you might be imagining. A baby wrapped in a fluffy, blue blanket wasn't delivered into our arms. Instead, we were taken into an office with a handful of doctors who didn't sugarcoat the situation.

Dr. S spoke first: "Understand that 50 percent of kids who leave with tracheostomy tubes die at home. You'll need to be 100 percent with him through this."

We both nodded. Nurses were scheduled to supervise Cornell for ten hours a day on our workdays, but in the end, Cornell's fate was on us.

Dr. S. continued, "I'd be remiss if I didn't seriously paint this picture for you before you go: Cornell is never going to walk, talk, or likely show any emotion. He will likely not ever be able to show any true love toward you. I don't want you to get your hopes up."

Kim grabbed my hand, and we both squeezed.

"Just know that we will give you all the help you need. If you decide to find an appropriate place for him down the line, let us know, and we will assist you in his placement."

A serious part of me wanted to stand up and scream, we *know! Can everyone please stop?* Instead, we signed the appropriate papers and walked out of the office. In the eyes of his Pulmonologist, we must have looked like fifteen-year-olds deciding to get married for no other reason than that we loved each other.

A few of the nurses walked us to our car. We were bundled in coats, as a light snow had begun to fall from the gray Virginia sky. Kim sat in the back seat with Cornell, and I headed to the driver's seat. At fifteen months old and about twelve pounds, this was the first time he had ever left the hospital. He sat in his car seat, facing backward. His breathing tube was connected to an oxygen tank that was wedged in between him and the front seat. The portable suction tube lay at Kim's feet. All of the other technology was loaded into the car, and a nurse who would accompany us home was up front, next to me.

I settled into the driver's seat and started the engine. "What did you think about what Dr. S said?" I asked her. I put the car into gear, and glanced in the rearview mirror, for the response. It came with extreme confidence.

"He's wrong."

—⁂—

Cornell was born at twenty-three weeks gestation, almost 4 months early on October 2, 1992 in Norfolk, Virginia. He weighed one pound, nine ounces. To give you context of how small he was, his physician said his wedding ring could easily fit over Cornell's wrist, and slide all the way up to his shoulder. To further complicate things, Cornell was a twin. His sister, Ariel, managed to do better medically, which is common; premie girls tend to do better than premie boys. They were both placed in the neonatal intensive care unit (NICU) at The Children's Hospital of the Kings Daughters. Cornell was put on a ventilator and feeding tube, and due to the chronicity of his condition, they put in a tracheostomy tube. The (NICU) would be his home for the first six months of his life.

Ariel fared better. She was able to return home with their family, and while we don't have all the information on the situation, we know that she would live with and be raised by her grandmother. The complexity of Cornell's condition was just too great for the family to tackle, and as time went on, the staff at Children's Hospital of The King's Daughters became his primary caretakers.

At six months old, Cornell was moved from the NICU to the Transitional Care Pavilion. TCP was an off-site ward for ventilator-dependent patients. Today, it's known as the Transitional Care Unit and is inside the hospital. It continues to treat some of the most chronically sick children at Kings Daughters. Many of these kids will never leave this unit. When Cornell arrived at TCP, he immediately began to receive care from a sharp, young occupational therapist. That young OT was my wife, Kim.

—✲—

After we decided to bring him home as our foster child (more on that later), it didn't take long for Cornell to come to life. In the first week, he seemingly only had a connection to Kim. I was terrified of him! Prior to bringing him home, we went through a daily, eight-week training process to practice taking care of his tracheostomy, gastric tube, and other medical issues. While I had become comfortable with all this at the hospital, it was now extremely intimidating to be 100 percent responsible when the nurses were not there. But, slowly, the daily care became routine, and what helped the most was Cornell's emerging, captivating personality. Within weeks, his infectious smile was lighting up the room, and unless something horrible was being done to him for medical reasons (which happened almost every day), he was just happy. In fact, I was amazed at how quickly he could calm himself down after one of those events, and how quickly he could find his happy place.

—ɯ—

During this period, Kim and I were able to continue working full time because the state provided nursing care for Cornell when we were gone. It also paid for eight hours of respite care per week, when a nurse would simply give the two of us a break. Cornell had professional physical therapy, occupational therapy, and speech therapy daily. When one of the therapists wasn't working with him, Kim or one of the nurses were. I pitched in as much as I possibly could. This was the beginning of "Team Cornell."

After months of work, Cornell's muscle strength and coordination improved, and he began to roll over. While this was a huge breakthrough, when it happened at night, his heart rate monitor would come unplugged, and the alarm would blare. Kim and I would race to his room, completely terrified of what we might find. Likewise, when Cornell came down with a cold, it was life threatening, many times sending him back into the hospital for a few days. Every development had us on pins and needles. We were in constant evaluation mode.

It was true that Cornell was a cause of stress, but the support and resources we had in place lightened the load a great deal. It felt less like work and more like a mission. This gave us the space to appreciate him. With the help, Kim and I fell in love with Cornell more each day. The most amazing part was the way he reacted to our affection. Smiling, rolling over, and making eye contact became daily accomplishments; his neural pathways were slowly developing. Cornell was coming to life.

Still, feeding him was a nightmare, at least for me. When a child is on his back for so many months with nothing in his mouth, the ability to swallow does not develop. Eating did not come naturally. Cornell just didn't know how to manipulate food, chew, or swallow. Trying to get a quarter ounce of anything into him would take over an hour, and he'd spend the majority of the time gagging, crying, and fussing. Kim's background in OT equipped her to handle the difficulty, and the nurses were pros. When I tried to feed Cornell, though, I felt like he was going to die. I just couldn't do it—and he knew it. It took him about four feeding sessions with good, old Dad to know that if he carried on and acted like he was in serious medical distress, I would cave and allow him to stop eating.

Kim would say, "John, he is playing you like fiddle."

I'd defend myself: "Kim, it's really serious this time!"

And then I would feed him though his stomach tube. Cornell would kick his feet and grin at this small victory. I soon lost my job as feeder, which, for the record, was fine with me. We all have our strengths.

For his part, our son didn't seem to like any food. Soon, however, we discovered he was willing to accept raspberry cobbler. But it wasn't as if it made him happy. One day, his primary nurse, Shirley, decided to give ketchup a try, and that was the game changer. He loved, loved, *loved* ketchup! When Kim arrived home, the nurse fed him some, so she could see his reaction. When I walked in the door, Kim had to show me, or I would never have believed it. A lot of ketchup was consumed, and Team Cornell walked a little lighter that day.

Because Cornell had a tracheostomy tube in place, he could not speak, or make any sound, for that matter. We began teaching him signs. I secretly didn't believe he would ever pick up on them. Unfortunately, the doctors' words kept ringing in my ears, even though Cornell had shown some positive growth. Loving him and believing in him were two separate entities.

Cornell had been with us for three months now, which put him at eighteen months. I can't remember where we were going that day, but I was carrying Cornell to the car in his car seat. I was with Kim, soaking up her smile and laughter. I opened the car door and plopped him down onto the front seat, which made a *clunk* sound. This, of course, made him laugh his silent laugh—his shoulders would bounce, and air would pass through his trach tube, never making it to his vocal cords, and make a raspy *hiss*, all accompanied by a big smile. But then he did something remarkable. Cornell brought his fingertips together and made the sign for "more."

I whipped my head around to see if Kim had seen it. She had—but we both were incredulous. Did we imagine it? I picked him up and *clunked* him down again. Sure enough, there came a bigger smile than before, a few kicks of his feet, and the physical request for more! He was grinning from ear to ear and looking at us out of the corner of his eyes. We were too stunned to tear up.

I felt like I'd been hit over the head. For the first time, I knew that the doctors were wrong, and that Kim had been right about Cornell all along. This kid's lights were on, and now he was communicating.

As the weeks went on, our boy became increasingly animated. To put it simply, he was just so happy. Cornell struggled to eat, sleep, crawl, and do anything normally; and, don't forget, the nurses and therapists were messing with him every day. He was enduring procedures that were often far from pleasant. Regardless of momentary discontent, Cornell would always find his way back to his quiet, happy demeanor. It was inspiring.

Suddenly, he was learning like crazy and picking up on words daily. In the blink of an eye, he had an entire vocabulary: Mom, Dad, birdie, please, thank you, eat, sleep, lion, hair, moon, sun, and so on.

At the four-month mark of Cornell being with us, we had a second bed put in the nursery to gear up for the arrival of Kaitlyn, our daughter who was due in June. We found out Kim was pregnant, a few weeks before Cornell came home. While our families were concerned about the magnitude of what we were about to tackle, Kim and I were committed to caring for Cornell, and we were beyond excited about our coming bundle of joy. With every rising sun, Kim was growing bigger, and we were preparing ourselves to have our colorful "twins." Let the games begin!

We still were not sure what the future would hold for Cornell. Our little foster baby was improving at light speed. Maybe the initial goal of getting him well enough to go home with his biological family would come true. That thought created a hollow pit in my stomach.

Little did I know that this sick little boy would teach me more than any other person in my life. The "effect" he would ultimately have on all of us would be immeasurable. He would change the trajectory of our lives.

1

KIM'S VISION

I was not blessed with the gift of faith. I was born in an Episcopalian home where my Mom, Barb, took me to church on most Sundays, while my dad, Colin, who lived with us prior to the divorce, went and played golf. It was clear that while my mother believed in something greater, my father did not. It had not always been like that.

The split came when one of my older sisters died at six years old. Wendy was mentally retarded and had been sent to a hospital in Toronto, overnight, for simple psychological testing. The cause of her death remains somewhat a mystery, but some think she may have been murdered by a psychotic nurse—one who was arrested for euthanizing children in the following years. The other explanation was a bowel obstruction. Nothing was being done to my sister that was invasive, she had nothing physically wrong, just simple psychological tests. This happened in the 1950s, a few years before I was born. At that time, explanations by people in power were simply accepted. It was a tragedy at the highest level, causing my mother to embrace her faith, and causing my father to separate himself from any entity that could allow something so awful to occur. Wendy's death would be the beginning of the end of my parents' marriage. My dad had checked out, but the divorce would not happen until I was eleven.

So, in my life, trying to have faith has been work. I find it fascinating that some of the most intellectual people have the least faith. I was certainly one of them. It took the combination of observing my wife's faith, watching how my in-laws lived, and witnessing the events of my son's life to remove all doubt when it comes to the existence of a greater being. When people ask me why we brought Cornell home, I simply state, "It was a God thing."

Around the same time that I opened my own dental practice, Kim started working as an occupational therapist at Children's Hospital of the King's Daughters. She'd received additional training to be able accept the position at the Children's hospital. It was an impressive job, because many of her young patients needed to recover from something quite serious.

Eventually, Kim found her niche in the ventilator-dependent area, the Transitional Care Pavilion. "TCP" had four pods, with four beds in each pod, so it housed sixteen patients, each with a frightening prognosis. Some were babies, some older, but most would struggle to survive at all. A team of nurses, doctors, and therapists like Kim would focus close attention on these kids. They were some of the best professionals in the world, in their area of expertise.

Now and again, I'd sweep into the hospital to visit Kim. I'll admit that a dentist's office has its own set of smells, but it cannot compare to that of a hospital. There was that sterile, sticky odor of plastic pill containers, and the smell of meatloaf from the cafeteria one floor below…. I didn't know how Kim did this each day. Couple that with the beeping sound of ventilators and the sound of footfalls on the lambent, white floor—some defeated, others frantic, most simply cautious. It was all too much for me, so I visited rarely.

But not for Kim. She'd come home every night with a sincere smile on her face and that overflowing *I love my job* expression. I suppose it gave her perspective.

As Kim and I devoted our time to our emerging professions, we also were ready to start a family. Kim had looked forward to becoming a mother her entire life. So, we started checking with home pregnancy tests, but days turned to weeks turned to months, with no success. All the failed attempts to become pregnant proved frivolous, and this began to tear at Kim's core. The children she worked with each day reminded her of all she had to be thankful for, though, even when she felt hopeless.

One day, I walked in the door from work, and Kim was finishing up a phone call. She didn't look at me but rushed to say goodbye to the person on the other end, and then sat on a chair in the kitchen, dejected.

The phone call was from a good friend of hers who'd gotten pregnant easily, seemingly overnight. My mind flashed to all the things that that couple would never have to go through, which we'd been enduring for months now—ovulation tracking, planned sex, the two-week wait when it was absolutely impossible not to be optimistic, no matter how many times we were burned… the negative tests following a visit to the bathroom, which meant it was once again official: there was no baby.

I was right there with Kim, selfishly envying that couple. It seemed to me a dizzy finger of fate had picked the couple to have a child, and it had no interest in pointing our way.

And then, one day, Kim was pregnant.

I suppose I'm making it sound like it all came together out of the blue after all our efforts, but no. We'd visited an obstetrician/gynecologist who walked us through various fertility treatments that were available during the early nineties. Kim was put on a drug called Clomid that would induce ovulation, thereby increasing her chances of conceiving.

JOHN C. CRANHAM, DDS

That morning, she rolled out of bed, holding her breath. I awoke to the sound of plastic wrap being ripped open and knew she was taking a test.

"John!" she sounded frantic. I sat up immediately, ready for another letdown. She plopped down on the end of the bed. "What does this look like to you? Is that a second line? *Do you see two lines?*"

I rubbed my eyes to try to get a clear vision. Just barely visible was a second pink line; but it was there. "Yes! That's a second line!" Kim jumped on top of me, tears and kisses all mixed up between us. She went to the doctor later that day to confirm the good news.

Kim glided to work that day, with her head in the clouds. She was filled with thoughts of, *Is this real? Am I imagining all of it?* But she knew the kids in her unit needed her full attention and did her best to focus.

A six-month-old had recently transferred from the NICU to Kim's TCP, and he was in rough shape. The little guy had been born October second, weighing in at a little over a pound.

There had been drugs in his system, and the initial family involvement had waned. His ventilator was hooked up to a tracheostomy tube in his throat, and a feeding tube was in place. The Doctors notes described a dismal prognosis, although the kid continued to push through each day and managed, months later, to be transferred to Kim's unit.

She hovered over him, watching his chest rise and fall with the vent he was attached to—a stark contrast to the growing life inside of her. She told me it made her commit to the premie who had to rely on her and the accomplished team for everything, even breathing. At six months old, he wasn't much bigger than a newborn. "And your name is,"—she checked her paperwork again—"Cornell. Alright, Cornell. We can do this." Already, the little guy had drawn her to him.

The following weeks were blissful. Kim and I would come home from work at night, still overwhelmed with our good news.

"Should we tell Shannon?" she asked, speaking of her friend who had been maid of honor at our wedding.

"I don't know. Is it time to tell people?" I put my hand on her slim stomach. It defied my logic that something, a human, was growing in there.

"People say, don't say anything until the end of the first trimester. But how in the world can we wait that long? I'm a horrible liar."

"We've told our families. How about we leave it at that for now?" I suggested.

"Makes sense. How was the office today?" she said, leaning her head on my shoulder.

—⁓—

We never made it to the first ultrasound.

What words are there? Too much runs through a body with a loss like a miscarriage. This was also long before social media, and it seems to me, if we'd had the opportunity to read in blogs and posts how common it was to lose a baby, especially in the first trimester, it might have helped slightly. Instead, Kim, in particular, felt alone, and spiraled into a dark place.

Her only solace, for some time, was work. When she couldn't communicate her sadness to me or anyone else, she found herself talking to her kids.

"Good morning, Cornell. How's my little man?" She hovered over his bed. At that point, Cornell was a few months away from being one year old, and with each week the chance of weaning from the ventilator, and recovering, decreased. Kim figured he'd already defied the odds by making it this far, so *who knew?* She felt like it was her job to believe in these kids.

She started her therapy with him and tried to keep her mind from wandering to her own sadness, but that was awfully hard. "Cornell, I cannot believe someone out there is your mom, and she isn't here checking on you every day."

And then it happened. It was like Cornell wanted my wife to focus on something other than the events of the past many months. Kim returned to work, to hear her coworkers talk about how he was beginning to wean off the ventilator. It is important to recognize that one of the primary goals for the team at TCP is to get the kids off the vent. The children with muscular dystrophy have very little chance to do so, and while Cornell's diagnosis was stark, they still maintained hope, and worked diligently. Perhaps their skill, combined with Cornell's fighting instincts, could give him a shot.

The supervising nurse gave her the good news. "Dr. S thinks he is ready. We have decreased his ventilator settings. Just keep an eye on him, but it shouldn't preclude you from doing your normal stuff." The nurse was beaming.

Kim lifted his froglike legs and poised them above his body, frozen, as if to avoid jinxing this moment. And then she went through her normal routine, but with a level of hope and joy she had not felt in some time. She kept a close eye on his monitors through the session, and all key indicators stayed in the normal range.

She finished her therapy session with him. "You're a rock star!" she pronounced. She did a little dance right there in the TCP and then happened to run into Dr. S in the hall.

"I am so excited about Cornell's progress, his therapy session went great today." It was like she was trying to push along the protocol.

"He has a long way to go," he cautioned. "But so far so good. You know the drill. We will know more in a few weeks."

She got the message. Kim couldn't call herself the most unemotional individual at that time, so she lowered her expectations, perhaps to keep from another disappointment. At home that night, she didn't find it worth mentioning to me when we talked about our days.

Four days later they lowered the ventilator settings, and a few days after that they did it again. With each decrease Kim's demeanor changed. It was like the knob on that machine, was directly connected to Kim's outlook on life. I finally had to know what was going on.

What is going on with you? I see the spark back in your eyes?'

Kim blushed "My little guy at TCP is all of a sudden making great strides. The Pulmonologist has been weaning him off the ventilator, and it is going really well. We all just love him because he responds to us. There is something different about this one. I am just so happy for him. I have a great feeling about it."

In the weeks that followed, Dr. S carefully decreased the ventilator settings. With each decrease, Cornell responded appropriately. While his oxygen saturations might initially drop slightly, with time they would climb back into the normal range. He was fighting, and his body was adapting favorably. The team could not walk by his crib without smiling.

Kim was in the business of improvement, and while Cornell wasn't making large strides, he was moving forward each day, at a pace all his own. It was hard not to have a soft spot in your heart for him. It was great news for Cornell, but it was exactly what Kim needed in her life at the same time. Their two paths started to become inexplicably intertwined.

Each day Kim went to CHKD and worked with her Kids. She found herself spending a little more time with her favorite patient. Dr. S and the respiratory team continued their work. Then, on one glorious day he simply turned the vent off. I am sure there has to be some anxiety in that final moment. In this case, Cornell was now breathing with a gentle stream of oxygen flowing over his tracheostomy tube; with no help from the ventilator. Mission accomplished. This is what the special people (Doctors, Nurses, Physical Therapists, Occupational Therapists, Speech Therapists, Respiratory Therapists, and all the support staff) that work on units like this, live for. Cornell was on his way back.

That night at home, Kim had that bounce in her step I hadn't seen in quite some time. She couldn't stop talking about the miracle she had witnessed at work. I loved her excited voice and was filled with an old, familiar warmth.

It turned out that good news hardly ever comes without some bad news. If Cornell was breathing on his own, he'd need to move out of Kim's unit. There wasn't a bed for him elsewhere at Children's Hospital of the King's Daughters, so he was transferred to St. Mary's Infant Home in Norfolk, where there was space. The place was for profoundly retarded children, most with multiple medical issues from which they'd never recover. To their credit, it's a fantastic facility, but the primary goal is to care for chronically sick children that have little chance to improve.

Kim was livid, and she was not alone, several of her coworkers were upset. "How can they think Cornell belongs in a place like that?" While she had the greatest respect for St. Mary's, she worried about Cornell's prospects there. He would have zero chance to develop. "Look how much progress the two of us made! Clearly he's higher functioning than this!" She took her emotions out on the dishwasher as she unloaded it, slamming cabinets and cutlery every which way.

For about a week, that was all she could talk about, with me and anyone who would listen. While many of the nurses and therapists agreed with her, there just didn't seem to be any other options. The Hospital had policies and rules were rules. She realized her hands were tied.

Weeks passed. I was mashing together my chicken, rice, and broccoli when Kim put her fork down. Unlike me, she liked to keep her food separate in nice, neat groupings. She stared at her plate, and I waited for her to gather her thoughts. Finally, she said, "I can't get Cornell out of my mind."

"I know," I said.

Her eyes turned down, and she looked exhausted. "I can't help thinking"—she inhaled—"that maybe all this stuff we've been going through is for a reason." She rubbed her forehead with one hand. "I think we are supposed to bring Cornell home with us."

My beautiful Kim. How caring was that? She lifted her gaze from her plate and managed to look at me like a lost puppy hoping to be let inside.

I needed a minute. Actually, I needed a lot of minutes. Hundreds of thoughts zoomed through my head, and not one of them led me to want what Kim wanted. I'd seen the kids in the Transitional Care Pavilion. In some respects, they were intimidating, due to all they required. I needed to be honest in that I had no interest in becoming involved in this situation. "Kim, I love you, but I don't think we're supposed to do this." I went on to side with the doctors and how logical they were. "I'm sorry, but you can't save every sick kid at the hospital." She didn't attempt to interrupt all my rational thoughts on the subject. She just kept listening. "You might be comfortable around chronically sick kids with tracheostomy and gastric tubes, but I'm not."

I knew I'd hurt her somehow, but she didn't let on. Instead, she gracefully responded, "This is a decision that has to be made by both of us. And I understand you." She reached for my hand, and I gave it to her. "Really, I do."

The topic of Cornell was not brought up again for some time. Part of this was the magic of Kim, her patience and poise. Another part was that I didn't want to talk about it. I'd said my piece. Looking back, I now realize the massive elephant that hung out in the room with us, but at the time, we simply focused on going through the motions of our daily lives.

The weirdest realization was that Cornell was on my mind too. Constantly. I found myself thinking about him at work, in the car, and even in my dreams. Seriously, I was having dreams about a one-year-old boy I'd never seen before. And visions of a small, healthy, beautiful,

African American boy running on the beach. I hoped and prayed these visions would pass. I was most likely feeling guilt over my wife's request that I'd shot down weeks earlier.

Kim and I were at St. Therese Catholic Church one Sunday, like any other Sunday, and I was prepping for the priest's homily. Actively listening to a homily had never been a strength of mine. My mind would wander to anything and everything else. By the time it was over, I often couldn't tell you what the message was or how I might be a better person because of it. However, that day, Father Jim Griffin was speaking, I found myself engaged. He talked about the importance of listening carefully to God's quiet voice. "He will speak in many different ways to guide us on the path we are meant to take," he said. "Sometimes God's path may appear to be the difficult path, the less desirable path, the impossible path. But, following God's path will always have the greatest rewards."

Something stirred and knotted up within me. His message was tugging at me like a child tugs at an arm to get his dad's attention. No one else in the church existed aside from me and Father Jim—it was like he was speaking two inches from my face. I heard him, loud and clear, and the meaning plunged deep inside me.

He finished the message, and I was jarred from my trancelike state. I immediately turned to Kim, grabbed her hand, and said, "I think it's time we bring Cornell home."

And so, Kim and I put into motion the process of becoming Cornell's foster parents, because there didn't seem to be any other option. Interracial adoptions were frowned upon, and interracial foster situations were extremely rare, but we were granted the ability to do so as a last resort.

Off to the hospital we went. However, it was nothing like adopting a child. In that case, at least in the early nineties, a couple might receive a phone call from an adoption agency with which they'd submitted an application. The agency would interview them and say something vague like, "We'll be in touch," and that could mean anything at all. The couple would wait. And every time the landline would ring, they'd jump and think, "Is this it?"

And someday, after who knew how long, there would be a fateful phone call, with the person on the other end of the line saying, "We have a baby for you." The couple would grab the carefully assembled baby bag that had been accumulating dust in the back room. They'd put on nice clothes and call both sets of parents before starting the car. And all the way to the hospital, they wouldn't dare breathe or converse; that mother might still change her mind.

Kim and I weren't simply picking Cornell up because we received a green-light phone call. We'd have to complete an eight-week training program before that could happen. We went to the hospital to sign the initial papers, and so I could meet Cornell for the first time. We signed and were taken to the little bed to which he was attached.

"There's my little guy," Kim said, scooping up this teeny, tiny thing like she'd been doing it her whole life.

I, on the other hand, could hardly breathe. The air was caught in my throat. I'd been told all about Cornell, but to see him was a different thing entirely. He was Thirteen months old and weighed about nine pounds. You're probably Googling that right now, because it's almost impossible to picture what that looks like. He was hooked to multiple machines via tubes in his stomach and throat. Cornell didn't look like the baby I'd envisioned five minutes earlier when I signed my name. He reminded me of something from the movie *The Matrix*.

"Do you want to hold him?" Kim asked innocently.

"Next time," I said, grabbing his little hand. He seemed too fragile, and the thought of him being in my care made me nervous.

Kim picked him right up, and we saw the first sign of a personality from Cornell. His eyes stared in wonderment at her jewelry. "You like that?" Kim asked as he reached for her necklace. He also seemed fascinated by her hair and ID badge. He touched her ever so gently.

I stared at him and tried my hardest to see the spirit in his wandering eyes. But really, I was hanging on by threads, doing everything possible not to have a mild panic attack. All I could think of were my shortcomings—my supposed inability to care for someone who needed so much help.

What were we doing? The unknowns here were so great. But something stopped me, like a flashing barricade, from turning around and running toward the nearest exit sign. It was either God or Kim. If it were God, I didn't understand. If it were Kim, I knew I couldn't see the look on her face if I told her I couldn't be on board.

When Kim put Cornell down, he stopped making any sort of eye contact and showed an inability to roll over. Did he know all these people were watching him, waiting for him to perform? I wanted so badly to see beyond his exterior and know his inner workings. *If I could just see what Kim sees*, I thought.

We said goodbye and walked through the hospital, hand in hand. Kim was glowing. I was silent. Luckily, I didn't have to find any words.

"I know that was a lot," Kim said. "I realize I'm used to Cornell and have been with him for a while now." I nodded. "But keep the faith. I promise he won't seem so breakable and helpless when you start spending time with him."

"Okay." I smiled and squeezed her hand. I hoped she was right.

2

INSPIRED BY HIS FIGHT

She was right. It was a struggle, but soon the technology, the medical issues, all of it, felt routine. Even having an infant, Kaitlyn, in the routine felt pretty good. It was a joyous, busy, time. Cornell was reaching two years old, and everyone—me, Kim, the nurses, and the doctors—assumed he would have the tracheostomy tube removed because he'd be strong enough to breathe on his own. Usually, this is a simple matter of removing the tube and repairing the site. But at twenty months, we received some devastating news. The doctors found that Cornell's trachea had closed off just above the surgical site. The only way to get him to breathe on his own was to do a major surgery called a laryngotracheoplasty (LTP).

Dr. D, his ear, nose, and throat surgeon, described the plan. "We take cartilage from Cornell's ribs, create a vertical slit in his trachea, and splice cartilage into the walls of his trachea. The goal will be to create a normal-sized airway tube, above the tracheostomy site. Right now, it is completely closed off.

"The most difficult part of the process will be post-surgery," he continued. "Cornell will need to be kept completely still for a week following the procedure. We will keep him in intensive care, nasally intubated and asleep, until the grafts 'take.' This should last about seven days."

It sounded like an eternity.

"How long will this surgery be"?

"This is a procedure I do fairly often, and if all goes well, we are looking at an eight- to ten-hour procedure."

"Jesus," I muttered under my breath.

—⚋—

I vividly remember Cornell sitting on my lap at four-thirty in the morning on the day of the surgery. We had not left the house yet, and I was giving him a breathing treatment. Every five minutes, he would pass a little gas and absolutely crack himself up. He was such a happy, little guy, and I could not help but think that he had no idea what was just hours away. Kim and I were so frightened.

There really wasn't a decision to be made, so Cornell endured the ten-hour procedure. He made it through without issues, and every time he would wake up in the week to follow, the doctors would knock him out again. It was obvious he was in pain when his eyes would flutter open. It was a brutal time for Kim and me. The misery you feel when your child is hurting is like nothing else.

When the week was over, the doctors woke Cornell up, and immediately we could see that he wasn't himself. That light had gone out in his eyes. His smile was nowhere to be seen. Cornell just sat there. We did not know it yet, but something was very wrong.

The next seven weeks marked one of the most difficult time periods of my life. It wasn't abnormal then for Cornell to just stop breathing. He'd have to be bagged and put on oxygen immediately. Kim and I started forcing ourselves to continue our weekly date nights, even though it was clear the two of us were struggling emotionally. Neither of us slept; we lay there and simply waited for him to code.

One of those nights, we treated ourselves to our favorite entertainment, a James Taylor concert. The two of us pretended to be normal people for a few hours and, dare I say it, we sincerely had a good time. Cell phones were in their infancy, so after the concert we got back in the car, found a pay phone, and called home. Shirley's words were clear and concise. "Cornell has stopped breathing. I am bagging him, and the ambulance is on the way."

Nothing was said in the twenty-five–minute ride home from the Hampton Coliseum. I remember turning onto our street and seeing the flashing lights of the ambulance. Our friends Billy and Jennifer dropped us off, and Kim climbed into the back of the ambulance as the paramedics worked to stabilize Cornell. I got into my car and followed.

For whatever reason, the doctors continued to doubt that anything was actually wrong with Cornell. Something about "the nurse may have over reacted." The next day, they sent him home with us. We spent weeks rushing back and forth from our house to the hospital with Cornell, until the doctors finally agreed to give him a bed for observation.

At night, Cornell would experience spells of "respiratory depression," in which he would fight with everything he had just to breathe in and out. Kim and I would take turns with him each night, and on many occasions, I'd see his tiny chest race up and down—an awful pulling that exposed every rib in his chest.

When he wasn't in respiratory depression, he was lifeless. He sat there in complete silence, zero animation, with a completely blank look on his face. Dr. TM was one of the physicians monitoring his condition. He is a pediatric critical care specialist, and one of the most brilliant doctors with whom I have ever come in contact. He would spend hours standing at the end of Cornell's bed, watching him, studying the monitors, and making notes. It didn't matter if the boy were in an anoxic event, or sitting there listlessly, the physician was trying to figure out what was wrong. On one of those days, I was asking some tough questions.

"Dr. TM, where has our son gone? His laughter, his huge personality… what is going on with him?"

He responded, "There is something seriously wrong with your son. He is sensing impending doom. And I am going to figure out why."

That statement sent chills through my spine.

At home, Kaitlyn was just a baby, and if she were aware of Cornell's absence, she had no way of letting us know. She was an infant who needed love and care. So Kim and I started to split our time to give our best to both children. We worried that all the energy we were expending towards Cornell, was causing us to miss things with her. It was difficult not to feel guilty.

Our hope started to flicker. During one of my Cornell nights at the hospital, when he was fighting to breathe, his heart rate was between 180 and 200 beats per minute. It was too hard to watch, and for the first time, I had the concrete belief that he would not make it to morning. My insides knotted up. What was I to do? Just watch him? Like this?

Keep in mind we were in a teaching hospital. At night, residents were on call, dedicated doctors who were still doing their training and lacked a lot of experience. As the clock ticked to about three in the morning, I turned to one of the residents and told him I did not think Cornell was going to make it through the night. I demanded that he wake up a "real doctor, *now!*" Definitely not my finest moment, but I was desperate. So the resident went to make some phone calls and left me with my son, who was struggling to breathe, fighting for his life.

I picked up Cornell's hand and held it in mine. I started to pray. I'm certain none of it was coherent, but between my tears, I started to question why he was fighting so hard. Thinking that he had had enough. Essentially, I gave him permission to check out.

"You don't have to fight so hard buddy," I told him. "It's okay. I love you."

Behind my words, I was thinking that I wouldn't have the strength to push through this. If it were me, I would have been too weak and quit long ago. I was giving him permission to go be with God.

Cornell's hand twitched slightly. I looked up, red-faced and teary. Cornell's eyes were wide open, and he was looking directly at me. He took a big breath, closed his eyes, and stopped breathing. This is it, I thought. I began to lose my peripheral vision, as I thought I was about to pass out.

Ten seconds later, his eyes popped open. He looked away from me, but I could see he was fighting even harder.

In that magnificent moment... *I watched Cornell choose life.* I knew for certain, in the exact same circumstances, I would have quit. It's a realization that haunts me to this day.

This was a moment that would forever change me. With each labored breath Cornell took that night, I understood more fully that our gift from God is life—the whole package, the good and bad, the gifts and the disabilities. All of us have both, and it's a matter of what we do with what we're given. How hard will we fight?

Years later, Cornell's pulmonologist, would become my patient. He would come in for an exam and want to catch up on the progress of one of his favorite patients—Cornell. One day, after I spun my tale of my son's latest triumph, he shook his head and said, "I just love hearing about these kids.".

That stopped me short. "Wait," I said. "Are all of these kids from the NICU like this?"

To which he said, *"Only the ones that make it."*

He went on to explain that some people are just born fighters. This is not a gift that is given uniformly. Certainly, some kids are sicker than others, but the kids that have what Cornell was born with have only a small chance at survival. Medical care is obviously hugely important, but without the insatiable appetite for life, they just don't make it. He said he could almost look at the monitors of these premie babies and, within the first few hours, know the ones that have the fight in them.

"It's a trait that doesn't seem to go away as they grow; it is just hard-wired in them."

His words literally rang in my head.

After that magical night, I was determined to alter the effort and passion I would put into my own life. It occurred to me much later that, before Cornell, I was an 85-percenter. I had come into the world with some challenges, for sure, but with so many gifts. And I had figured out that by applying myself 80 to 85 percent, I could do pretty well. My stepfather challenged me on this early in my life, after a rather ordinary high school career: "give it 100 percent in college and see what happens."

Through college, I applied myself completely and received the rewards of that work, which got me into dental school. But now, as a young professional, I was drifting back. I was starting to feel successful enough that if obstacles were too great, I would accept rather than challenge them. This night changed all that.

I realized that Cornell's happiness and zeal came from the 100-percent mentality, having to give it his all just to survive. I was humbled, observing him, by the realization that I, too, have another gear to explore. It may not be hard-wired in me, but I was sure I could learn to be more like my son. How could I fight for my own life and livelihood, as Cornell did for his own?

After the longest seven weeks of our entire lives, the doctors finally listened to his mother, me, and the nurses. The grafts weren't working, so the decision was made to put the trach tube back in his throat. The surgery to do so went effortlessly, and Kim and I were so relieved. Just like that, our happy Cornell was back! He could breathe again! It turns out, oxygen is rather important.

Cornell slowly recovered once the tracheostomy tube was back in place. He continued to grow, gained some weight, learned more signs, and still pushed himself to keep up with Kaitlyn. We took a family vacation to the Virginia mountains when Cornell was thirty-two months old, and there, he finally took his first steps. To the thumping of Michael Jackson's "Beat It," Cornell wobbled back and forth across the room between Nurse Shirley and me as Kim videotaped him. Kaitlyn clapped and laughed, and occasionally went for a full-on tackle in the middle of the room. In no time at all, Cornell's walk turned into a run, and there was no stopping him. Way up high in the Blue Ridge Mountains, Cornell believed he'd conquered the world.

When you are young, it seems to me, you don't have the capacity to understand where another 15 percent of effort will take you. I can tell you that having this experience early in my career led me to places that I didn't think were possible: not only building a thriving dental practice that had me doing the kinds of procedures I dreamt of doing… but having patients occasionally fly in to see me for their care. I credit it with increasing my initiative to build a seminar business, which eventually allowed me to collaborate with my longtime mentor and write a textbook with him. I went on to create treatment planning software and, ultimately, teach dentists all over the world.

Had I stayed an 85-percenter, none of that would have happened. If you can learn to apply yourself to your full capacity—or near that mark—your life, income, and your way of living will be unrecognizable in five years. It is the juice that will create the life you are dreaming of.

3

FIRST STEPS AND OUR
FIRST GLIMPSE INTO HIS SOUL

Kaitlyn was born on June 17, 1994, a very important day in United States history. I say that with a heavy eye-roll. While Kim was in labor, we couldn't take our eyes off the television because the O.J. Simpson "slow-speed Bronco car chase" was on every other channel. Whether we want to or not, we'll never forget that.

We signed the letter *K* onto Cornell's right cheek and brought him to the hospital to see her that afternoon.

"Say hello to your sister, Cornell," Kim cooed.

That poor kid. He took one look at the baby in Kim's arms and burst into tears. He wouldn't even look at her! It still makes me chuckle. Luckily, his distress over Kaitlyn didn't last long. In fact, he was quickly captivated by his new little sister.

Our house was bubbling over with so much love, it was surreal to me. Of course, with two babies in the house—one newborn and one special needs—we were busy. It really was like having twins. When Kim's leave ended, she returned to work full time, which meant workdays lasting anywhere from eight to ten hours. Kaitlyn went to day care, and Cornell continued his routine with the at-home nurses.

We'd gained some continuity here, with Shirley as our primary nurse and Elise as our secondary. We had their help forty-eight hours a week. Thankfully, there was one night a week built in so that Kim and I could go out, just the two of us. Needless to say, Cornell couldn't be left with a run-of-the-mill babysitter.

In those first months, Cornell was way ahead of Kaitlyn. He was smiling and signing and overall kicking butt. However, in the blink of an eye, Kaitlyn caught up developmentally. At eight months, she was signing right along with Cornell.

Our kids shared the same bedroom, and I could only imagine all the childlike ways they communicated across their cribs. These days, there are video monitors that allow you to watch your children from another room. If those were available then, I'm sure we would have enjoyed following their shenanigans. I can clearly remember one night when I walked into their room to say goodnight, and they were standing up in their cribs, laughing at each other and throwing toys back and forth. They were two peas in a pod.

When Kaitlyn started talking, it was like she'd transformed into a mythical creature before Cornell's eyes. He was fascinated by it because, keep in mind, he still couldn't make a sound. He loved everything about her talking. Each time she would learn a new word, he would smile, clap, and laugh. No one was a bigger fan of Kaitlyn than Cornell.

The two of them learned to pull up on things to stand, no problem. One day, Cornell pulled himself up to look out a window, and Kaitlyn began a frantic crawl to cross the room and join him. Suddenly, in the center of our living room, Kaitlyn popped up and finished her journey on her two feet. Cornell was so excited, he fell over backward, clapped, and kicked his feet.

How to describe a paradoxical moment like this? We were thrilled for our daughter—what an incredible moment! But it hammered home the fact that she was miles ahead of Cornell. At that point, it would still be quite a few more months and hours of physical therapy before

Cornell would take his first steps. Our hearts felt full and compressed at the exact same moment. Kim and I did our best to focus on Cornell's demeanor as Kaitlyn checked off more accomplishments. He was her biggest cheerleader every step of the way. It also seemed like Kaitlyn motivated Cornell to work even harder. There wasn't room to be sad about Cornell falling behind. He was too joyous to allow it.

—⁂—

Comparison is the enemy of contentment, something Cornell clearly seemed to understand. You will see countless examples of this one trait throughout Cornell's story: the ability to be happy for those around you. Carefully watch for them. I maintain this may be his greatest gift, the ability to appreciate others' gifts. Even when they develop faster, have more, or are just ahead of you. The ability to not feel jealousy. The ability to not compare. The ability to not have a story in your head about where you should be, based on some arbitrary time frame. The ability to grow, develop, and ultimately, succeed at your own pace.

It is amazing when you really think about it. There were so many opportunities for him to have felt sorry for himself. But he just didn't. Some people may think that he didn't have the intellectual capacity to see that he was falling behind. That is not the case. He was extremely aware … and he was genuinely happy for others' gains. Most of us lose enormous chunks of time, we lose amazing opportunities, because we are busy thinking and comparing ourselves to those around us. It's tough to do but STOP IT!

4

SEEKING OUT GREAT COUNCIL TO WEATHER THE CHALLENGES AHEAD

As time ticked away, the connection between Cornell and our family grew stronger. We began thinking more and more about adopting him. Biracial adoptions were not common in Virginia in 1994, so we knew challenges would lie ahead. We also had so many concerns about parenting him, beyond just the medical challenges.

"At what point do we tell him about being adopted?" Kim asked. "I realize he is a different race, and eventually he will know, but do we just wait, or do we talk about it?"

I didn't answer. "What about all the medical issues he has endured at such a young age? I have read that kids may not to be able discern between physical abuse and procedures like this. And what about the fifteen months he was in the hospital? I know you all were loving him, but he wasn't in the home. Will there be attachment issues? Are we ready for the personality stuff that is likely to start coming out as he grows up?"

These conversations popped up periodically, and my anxiety grew. Then, one day, Kim heard a name, we will refer to as Dr. W. She is a brilliant child psychologist who was at the same Children's Hospital. Kim suggested we go meet with her, to get ahead of some of the things we were concerned about. I loved the idea. So, calls were made, schedules were aligned, and we set out for our first visit.

After exchanging pleasantries, Dr. W. let us know she had done some research and knew Cornell's history. She also told us she thought what we were doing was incredible. She had a positive energy that was pulling me in.

"How is he doing now?" she asked, "How is he developing?"

Kim replied, "He's doing really well. He had all those issues with the first surgery, as you know. But his fun personality is back. He is learning new signs almost every day. He can't walk yet, but he is crawling and scooting all over the place. He continues to get PT, OT, and Speech almost daily, and he just works so hard."

Dr. W. sat there smiling as Kim talked and filled her in on further details. "That is incredible. Honestly, with his history, a twenty-three–weeker, the time in the hospital… you realize those things probably shouldn't be happening."

"Yeah, we have heard," I said, chuckling.

We were both sitting there, beaming with pride.

"So, what can I help you with?"

We spent the next fifteen minutes talking over our concerns. We wanted to know when and how to tell him about the adoption. How we were going to deal with the racial differences. Strategies for dealing with his learning issues. Sitting across from us in a leather chair, she took notes and asked for clarification on certain points. Dr. W was one of the best listeners I had ever met. During our conversation, we learned that she married a man from a different race and had biracial children, so she could speak to us from both a professional perspective and her personal experience. Then she was quiet for a long time, and just studied her notes.

Then she spoke.

"If you decide to adopt Cornell, you need to start talking about these things immediately. You can decide how to do this, but maybe you show pictures of Kim pregnant with Kaitlyn, and then you can start telling Cornell he was in another woman's tummy. Remember, to kids under five, this is just information. You are also telling him the truth. The earlier he hears this, the better. After the age of five, children begin to develop their sense of self. Their own identity. Trust me, I see kids like this where this one factor can be the root of many problems in an older child. Finding out they were adopted at that point in time can create real issues for them."

I must have been sitting there with a weird look on my face. She continued, turning her attention specifically to me.

"I know what you are thinking. Don't wait for him to figure out he is a different race and must have been adopted. It sounds amazing, but kids don't know that a color difference necessitates a different set of parents."

I nodded.

"The second thing I would say, along that same vein, is to talk openly about race. Again, it sounds crazy, I know, but children may not notice the differences for a long time. And once they realize they are different it can have a similar effect on their sense of self."

She held our gaze. Then Kim asked, "What do we do when race becomes an issue? Like, if a little kid says something to Cornell or our kids when they are playing. How do we deal with that?"

"Well, first of all that will happen. Don't think it won't." She smiled softly. "But that is why you are here. We are going to get you ready for that." "Let me give you a real-life example," she continued. "As I told you, my kids are biracial. My children have darker skin then I do. I came in the house one day, and one of my children was in the bathroom, with the water running for a very long time. I went into the bathroom and saw my daughter washing her hands over and over vigorously. I inquired what was going on and found out that they had been teased about being 'darker' than everyone else. She was trying to wash the color off."

Kim and I were silent.

"What I did that moment was to let the child know, in no uncertain terms, that God makes his children exactly as he intends. In his eyes, I told her, you are perfect."

Now Kim smiled. "Brilliant!" she said.

Dr. W went on. "Exactly. Do not get caught up in the conversation of which color is better, different shades, and all the other things they might hear. Talk about race early, and make sure they know that God made them exactly as he intended. Perfect in his eyes. All our kids need to hear this early and often, and it will provide them all with some armor as they move forward in life." She said this with the certainty that they would need it.

She said quietly, "One of the things you need to remember is, no matter how hard you try, neither of you will know what it is like to be a black man in America. Your son is going to have different experiences than you have. He will experience bias and racism. It will be harder, and one of your responsibilities as a parent is to get him ready. Life will be difficult for your daughter in this sense, and any other kids you may have, as well. The best defense is to build an emotionally strong person. This is not easy, but I can help you with that."

We let this sink in for a minute, and then Kim asked, "Do you think we are crazy for doing this?"

It was a very good question. I was secretly glad I was not the one who asked it.

She laughed. "Yes. You have both completely lost your minds! Seriously, of course not. This is all doable. Are there challenges? Yes! However, every parent will tell you there are rough waters with every child that they have. In this case, you just have an idea of what some of those challenges may be."

Kim and I were starting to feel better. And then, Dr. W's expression changed, and she became a bit more serious. "There is something you have yet to bring up that is your greatest challenge. It supersedes the issue of race or being adopted," she said in a leading tone.

"What the heck is that?" I asked.

"It is the issue of being a parent to a disabled child. Cornell has been given a ridiculously difficult hand. He was born three and a half months early and will likely feel abandoned by his birth family. Drugs were in his system, he spent fifteen months being raised by a hospital, he has been placed with a family of a different race. The boy has major developmental issues, and likely some level of brain impairment— although clearly not as severe as he probably should have."

"We get all that. What is your point?" Kim asked.

"My point is, you both love this child; that is clear. You are both good people or you wouldn't be doing this. But you cannot treat him any differently." And then she dropped the bomb that has guided us through his whole life: "The sooner he learns that life is not fair, the better off he will be."

"Ugh. That sounds heartless," Kim said.

"It does, doesn't it?" Dr. W. addressed her. "Kim, remove your Mom hat and put on your occupational therapist hat. If someone breaks a leg and tears ligaments, it would be far easier to just carry that person everywhere. Right? But we both know that does not return this person to health. Physical and occupational therapy often involve some pain. Unfortunately, it's the only way."

"So, with Cornell, your most difficult challenge is going to be raising him with the same rules and regulations you impose on your other children. Do not cut him any slack. He will learn to use his issues to manipulate you both, to get what he wants, or avoid things he does not want to do."

Kim glanced in my direction. "We are already seeing some of that when John feeds Cornell," she said, laughing.

I stepped in. "Well, in my defense, it sounds like he is dying!"

"But he isn't, is he?" Dr. W. was not laughing. "He is manipulating you," she pointed out. "This is a great example. If it were up to you, he might never eat! Is that what you want?"

Then she smiled, and we all laughed.

"Now, it may be that you just can't stomach that, and John, there may be other times where you can jump in where it's difficult for Kim to do some things. You need to work as a team, and you need to provide checks and balances for each other. Moving forward, it is totally okay for you to feel compassion for your son, but don't feel sympathy. Never pity him. Help him completely accept who he is. The earlier he does that, the sooner he can start getting on with his life."

—◇◇◇—

Dr W's insights became a guiding light for us. Our sessions together gradually produced an informal handbook on how, we hoped, to be better parents. It's funny; you have to take classes to drive a car, but anyone can have and raise a human. It was not always easy, but we began implementing her strategies immediately. Not only with Cornell, but with Kaitlyn, and eventually, with our youngest daughter, Kristen, as well.

In later years, "life is not fair" became a mantra in our household. What is most interesting is that Cornell seemed to have the least difficulty in understanding the basic concept.

Time after time, Kaitlyn or Kristen would get into trouble and have a full-blown meltdown. *"That's not fair!"* they would scream.

I would just turn to Cornell, who would be sitting back and watching events unfold, and I would say, "Tell her, Corn."

"Life's not fair," he'd recite. Then came that quizzical, knowing grin. Occasionally, he liked to stick it to his know-it-all sisters.

—◇◇◇—

When I think back on Cornell's life, there is no question that the time we spent with the brilliant child Psychologist was invaluable. Her message not only taught us to be better parents, but it also helped us deal with our own stuff. She was right: life isn't fair. Gifts and obstacles are not distributed evenly. While, as a society, we need to work hard to fight injustices and work to create as level a playing field as we possibly can, in the end, the hand we have been dealt is all we have. What we do with our lives has to do with how we show up every day and play that hand.

When we were going through all of this, Colin Powell released his book, *In His Own Words*. He was the first African American U.S. secretary of state, and his rise to this position through the 1960s, '70s, and '80s had to be quite a story. I heard he was coming to our area for a book signing, so I went over to buy the book and get it signed. Something I could give Cornell when he was older.

I stood in the ninety-minute line, got a quick handshake and a signature, and read the book. It is a helluva story. There is one moment that stood out to me.

Powell had just received orders to go to a base that was south of the Mason-Dixon line. Keep in mind, this was the 1960s. Colin was raised in the North, in a racially diverse neighborhood. He had been active in sports and joined the military primarily because he believed that his hard work would be rewarded with advancement, more so than in the private sector. As an athlete, ability, not race, had led to the best person playing. He had placed himself in environments where racism was not right in his face.

When traveling through a Southern state, he stopped at a restaurant to get a meal. Upon entering the establishment, he was told he was not welcome, but if he liked he could order something and pick it up around back. I don't remember if he got the meal or not, but I remember the description of how he felt. He was angry, hurt, devalued, and devastated. And then the amazing part: he decided right then and there, he would never let another person make him feel like that about himself again. It was like he flipped a switch. The strength in being able to do something like that is incredible. It is also probably a big reason he became a leader in our country.

As I thought about Cornell, after leaving Dr. W's office, I couldn't help but wonder if our son was not wired with a similar strength. And with Dr W's help, maybe we could bring it to the surface.

5

ADOPTING OUR SON

When the sun came up, after the night we nearly lost him, I knew I was all in. The little boy who had very minimal means of communicating to me, had shown me his heart. He'd fought harder than any other human being I had ever seen. A constant reminder to us all, that telling someone you are going to do something, and showing someone that you are actually doing it, are two very different things. Cornell was walking the talk, fighting at a level I did not know was possible. If Cornell would fight this hard, I would exhaust all my resources to give him every opportunity. As a leader in my business, this is a lesson I have played over and over in my mind. The constant internal question, "Am I really leading by example, or am I just telling people what to do?" keeps me grounded. We didn't know it yet, but Kim and I had some choppy waters ahead. Cornell pulled us into his boat at the right time.

—~—

A little over a year after Cornell's first LTP surgery, Kim and I had to gear up for them to attempt it again. To say we were nervous wouldn't do it justice. We knew Cornell needed the trach removed, but we could hardly bear the thought of putting him through such pain, yet again.

The hospital called us in one day, and we assumed it was to discuss his upcoming surgery. To our surprise, one of the doctors said, "I want you to be aware we are making efforts to let Cornell's biological family know about his improvements."

I could feel the anxiety welling up in Kim.

"We have to follow protocol here. They haven't shown any interest in Cornell so far, but now that he's come such a long way, it might be a different story. Remember, this was our goal all along."

Once back in the car, Kim asked. "What do we do? I know it is what we intended, but he feels like ours now, doesn't he?"

"Yes, completely."

I couldn't imagine my life without him. To say we felt helpless was an understatement.

Kim and I were his parents. We had loved and cared for him as intently as if he were our own. We were frustrated by the lack of interest from his biological family. We had no idea what challenges they faced, but how could there have not been any interest up to now?

Then, one day, there seemingly was some interest. Someone in the family was inquiring about Cornell. We knew they couldn't simply drive up to the house and take him from us. But the law could. And by law, Cornell was our foster child, and not legally ours.

The next few days were tense. There was nothing for us to do but wait to hear something. And then the call came in: Cornell's biological family still wasn't interested in regaining custody. While a small part of us was sad that he wasn't wanted by those who shared his blood, we got over that very quickly.

Kim and I decided to adopt Cornell. I had made a promise to him and myself on that critical night, that if he could fight that hard to stay alive, I would use all my resources to give him a shot at a good life. I had been all in for quite some time, but now I wanted to make it official. We didn't wish for this type of scare again, that he might leave our family forever. We wanted Cornell to legally be our son and Kaitlyn's brother.

At that time, crossing the racial line in The Commonwealth of Virginia was still highly controversial. But it was the mid-nineties, for Pete's sake! I was fully aware of the looks and whispers my family absorbed everywhere we went but figured that was a social issue more than a legal one. Apparently, they went hand in hand.

I sought the council of an attorney friend, Earle Mobley. I met him early in my career. He became a great patient of mine, and he went on to have an amazing career of his own. Working in private practice, he became a highly sought-after defense attorney, and was elected as commonwealth's attorney for the City of Portsmouth in 2001. With dignity and distinction, he served the city, prioritizing public integrity investigations and difficult murder cases. The honor and skill with which he carried out his duties paved the way for his appointment as juvenile and domestic relations district court judge in 2014. Throughout his career, his focus was on what was right, and not on what was politically expedient. He was just what we needed. We didn't realize it at the time, but we had a pit bull as an attorney, and he was joining Team Cornell to make our son part of the family.

Earle made it clear that to make this happen, it would have to take place in the right Virginian city with the right judge. Without progressive thinking, Cornell might not be granted to us.

"I'll be sure all the ducks are in a row," our friend assured us.

He navigated the political waters beautifully. Earle recommended that we focus on getting this adoption granted in the City of Chesapeake. Over the course of four months, all went according to Earle's grand plan. He got us lined up on the right day, with the right judge. At last, Cornell Cranham was official! It would be one of the first biracial adoptions in the state of Virginia.

Sadly, in 2017, in his mid-fifties, District Court Judge Earle Mobley lost a long battle with cancer. Literally hundreds attended his funeral. In the back sat Kim, Cornell and me. Almost no one knew what he had done for us. That was the kind of guy he was, quietly making a difference in the world. I miss him and will be forever grateful.

With all we'd endured thus far, we felt extremely blessed that Cornell's adoption had gone through without a hitch. We threw a party at our house to celebrate. Our families and friends came together and celebrated the moment. Personally, I didn't realize how heavily Cornell's fate weighed on me until that day when I knew he wasn't going anywhere. I felt a freedom I hadn't realized was missing before.

—∽∽—

Not long after his adoption, it was time for Cornell to have surgery again. His procedure took longer, between eleven and twelve hours, but he would only have to remain asleep for a few days this round. The day the doctors woke him up, Kim and I were prepared to see the same beat-up, exhausted kid we'd seen the last time. We'd put on our thick armor and were ready.

We walked into the intensive care unit and heard someone squealing. I caught Kim's face in my peripheral vision. *What in the world?* We picked up our pace, rounded the corner to his bed, and there was Cornell with a big smile on his face, delirious over the noises coming out of his mouth. We were hearing our favorite guy for the very first time. In the past, when air couldn't reach his vocal cords, we'd rely on his facial expressions, tears, and body language to identify his emotions. We knew he was laughing or crying, but his trachea was closed, so we couldn't hear it. But now...

Cornell. Was. *Loud!*

When he woke up that morning, he had a signing vocabulary of about two hundred words. By the end of the day, he was already shaping some basic words together verbally.

One of those words was "Daaaaddy." Kim was furious. LOL.

—⚏—

Cornell's innate "leadership abilities" and his insatiable appetite for life would create a fierce connection with his sister, who I am convinced would have followed him to the end of the earth. He was just fun to be around. It also created a bond that many times we could see through a ridiculously strong, protective instinct in her toward her brother. There were countless times she went toe to toe with bigger kids, often boys, in defense of her brother.

The first time we witnessed this, Cornell was about five and Kaitlyn about three, while we spent a family day at the beach. The kids were making sandcastles while Kim, myself, and the extended family soaked up the sun. A few other kids were playing a ways down the beach, when one little boy broke from his group to beeline for Cornell. He marched up to our son, pushed him over, and snatched the shovel straight out of his hands.

I started to rise up from my beach chair, but before I could do so, Kaitlyn jumped up from her sandcastle and pushed the thief to the ground. Then she started to clobber him! Her arms were pinwheeling all over him. He had to have been two years older and six inches taller, but my three-year-old was beating the crap out of him. I pulled her off the now blubbering bully and forced her to apologize.

A bizarre set of emotions raced through my being. The bigger kid looked literally terrified of my young daughter as I held her back. I felt scared, proud, anxious, and embarrassed all at the same time. But it turned into outright laughter when I glanced over at Cornell, who was watching all this unfold. All I could see was teeth. His grin was from ear to ear, and it was aimed directly at his sister.

6

CARVING A PATH THROUGH HIS ELEMENTARY SCHOOL YEARS

Cornell was technology free for the first time ever. A few months after his second LTP procedure, the doctors surgically closed his G-tube site, and he was a wild man! Running, jumping, laughing, falling, talking—he was doing it all. It occurred to me he'd been happy his entire life, but now that he was feeling well, he was full speed ahead like never before.

Christmastime wiggled its way into our busy lives, and Cornell was abuzz. The lights and colors and "Happy Holidays" everywhere we went had him chatting up a storm. We typically spent Christmas Day at the Kelley's, with Kim's family, and this year was no exception. As far as we could tell, the entire clan was eager to spend the holiday with healthy, happy, trach-less Cornell.

Kaitlyn was developmentally a world beyond Cornell at this point, but the two of them took it in stride. She was walking and talking on a level he strived to meet, yet he had a long way to go. Cornell still relied on signing for most of his communication. I could watch the two of them interact until the cows came home.

That Christmas morning, our two toddlers were loopy with all the presents they received. Kim's brothers, Brian and David, bought Cornell his first basketball hoop. We opened it and put it together right away, giving Cornell and Kaitlyn a mini basketball and showing them how to throw it through the hoop.

Kaitlyn tried first, but the ball didn't have a chance of making its way to the basket. Everyone cheered for her anyway. Brian handed her the ball and said, "Try again, Kaitlyn. You got it this time."

Before she could chuck it, Cornell burst through the moment. He seized the ball, lifted it over his head, and threw it in a perfect arc. The ball made contact with the backboard and fell through the net. Not one of us expected that to happen, and I'm certain our mouths were open so wide, he could probably have tossed the ball into one of them.

In our shocked silence, Cornell screeched—in the best way—and ran over to slap me five. I handed him the ball to do it again, but he stopped and put his hand to his cheek, making a sign for Kaitlyn.

He wanted her to have a turn.

What three-year-old kid does *that*?

On Christmas morning, when most children in the world are selfishly ripping open gift boxes and tallying up "what they got," Cornell was only thinking of his sister. Brian and David lifted Kaitlyn up to the hoop, so she'd make a few baskets, but Cornell hit bucket after bucket on his own. With every basket, he signed Kaitlyn, making sure she had her moment of glory too.

I often try to put myself in Cornell's shoes, but it's a challenge. How must he have felt, knowing he was out of the woods? The only thing I truly understand is that Cornell's great joy was born from having great challenges. One of his most precious gifts could, perhaps, be his horrible initial circumstances. Kim and I would have understood if he'd wanted to sit in a corner and wallow in his misery. Shoot, we would have joined him! But Cornell chose, all on his own, not to do that. He didn't seem to want to spend time feeling sorry for himself.

There was too much fun to be had! And, man was Cornell fun. He was always cracking himself up, and that made us laugh too. He radiated a sense of complete contentment, and it was infectious.

On February 20, 1997, our second daughter, Kristen, was born. I have vivid memories (and video) of Cornell and Kaitlyn, the day before Kristen came, talking to her through Kim's belly. By now, Cornell had kicked sign language to the curb.

"Hello, Kwwisten! I wuv you! *See you tomorrow!*" he screamed.

Then we had three in diapers—a newborn, and two attempting to potty train. We were a different kind of busy than when Cornell was young, but nonetheless busy. Now that Cornell was technology free, we no longer needed the nursing help, so we very much felt like a busy, "normal" family. Kim and I made sure to continue our once-a-week date nights, but our most joyous times were the ones spent with our three awesome kids.

As soon as Cornell was old enough to walk and talk, we made sure he could shake hands properly. We practiced excellent eye contact and a firm introduction. "Hi, I'm Cornell," with a *shake, shake, shake*. It was important that our kids demonstrated proper manners.

I didn't anticipate how easy such a task would be for Cornell. Most young children are intimidated by introducing themselves to strangers, but Cornell did this as eagerly as eating ketchup. When our family walked into a restaurant for dinner, we would most certainly be greeted by stares in one form or another—people trying to make heads or tails of our family. However, any split-second of eye contact, and Cornell would be marching up to said person with his hand out: "Hi, I'm Cornell!" I privately became concerned about a potential future in politics!

In no way did we intend for this to be funny, but it couldn't help amusing us. Anytime we would find ourselves in a new environment, off Cornell went to introduce himself to the gawkers. Kim and I would watch people's look of disdain melt away when an adorable little boy looked them in the eye and wanted to shake hands. Suddenly, that person was smiling and looking up at us with an "I'm impressed" face.

Cornell's extroverted, social nature came naturally; we only gave him the tools to use it to the best of his ability. By letting Cornell be himself, people fell in love with him, and many started to pull for him in a way I'm sure they didn't expect. Not only that, but I believe this is one of the traits that helped people accept our family for who we were.

When it was time for elementary school, Kim and I had some decisions to make. Kim was raised in the Catholic school system and was a strong believer in it. I had no problem with that, but we quickly realized such a path probably wouldn't be best for Cornell.

Private schools receive the majority of their money from donations, whereas public schools are given money by the state. In some respects, it's a backwards system. Private schools are typically expensive, and yet, they don't have the resources the public schools do. Obviously, that's not the case for all.

We understood the education system more fully with Cornell. Early on, we knew the local Catholic schools hadn't the resources to provide our son with the tools he needed to be successful, like the public school would. However, Kaitlyn would have all she needed to thrive from the Catholic schools. After much discussion and weighing of the pros and cons, we decided Cornell and Kaitlyn would attend different schools. Kaitlyn would begin at a Christian-based nursery school called Portsmouth Catholic Elementary at that time, whereas Cornell would attend our neighborhood public school.

Cornell's new school was close to our house and had a wonderful program for learning-disabled children at preschool age. No matter what you hear, there's always that *I hope this goes okay* feeling when your child sets out on new terrain. So Cornell was lucky enough to have had a year of school with other special-needs kids prior to entering kindergarten. At two, he went to a place called DAC Center that provided therapy. We called it his "school" because he and a nurse would be picked up by a school bus to get there.

Kim and I pulled into the parking lot. "You ready, buddy?" I asked. "Ready!" Cornell exclaimed.

Kim and I helped him out of the car, and we each held one of Cornell's hands as we walked him to the platform in front of the preschool door. Parents and children alike were full of nerves. The teacher opened the door with a wonderful, "Good morning. Come on in!" Some children started to tear up, or worse, when mothers led them to the door and said goodbye. Others turned to their parents and said something like, "See ya!" and waltzed through the doorway. One of the good things about the first day of preschool was that everyone was so wrapped up in their own children, they didn't really notice the makeup of our family.

I wasn't sure what Cornell would do. If anyone was going to cry, it was more likely going to be Kim or myself. However, Cornell had already had experiences like this in the past.

We walked him over to the young woman in the pale-green cardigan. "Cornell, this is your teacher, Ms. M. If you have any questions today, you can ask her, and she'll help you," Kim said.

"Hi, Cornell." The teacher put out her hand. She was beating Cornell at his own game.

"Hi, Ms. M." He smiled back.

"We'll pick you up in a few hours. We love you, buddy," I assured him. Kim and I both embraced him and walked back to the car. Neither one of us looked back. Instead, we hoped he was about to have his best day yet.

Later, Kim picked up Cornell and spoke with his teacher. Apparently, he shed no tears that day and was incredibly cooperative.

Over the next few weeks, we met Cornell's other teachers, in music, gym, and art, and it was like we'd known them for years. Kim and I were at ease knowing Cornell was in the best hands possible each day. He learned to socialize and put together fundamental building blocks that would allow him to progress up the educational ladder. It was wildly fulfilling to watch our kids take in all they'd been learning. Not only that, but we knew both of them were having fun in the process.

About this time, Kim made the decision to cut her work hours to two days a week. This was a special time for Kim and Kristen. As Kaitlyn and Cornell headed off to school, Kristen was being driven all over town as a ride-along, to keep up with the comings and goings of our new students. During the day, things were a little quieter, and it gave Kim and Kristen some very special time together.

One of my favorite memories from this period is when the students came together for a Christmas concert in December. Cornell's class was given a song to sing with sign language to accompany it. I don't know what motivated his teachers to include the sign language, but Cornell was thrilled. We practiced so much that even Kaitlyn was absent-mindedly singing the lyrics throughout the house.

I cannot tell you how fun it was to see Cornell perform with his classmates at the concert. We left our folding chairs and crowded in front of the stage with all the other preschool parents trying to snap the best picture. Kim mouthed the words to keep Cornell on track, and he hit it out of the park. The entire night was a success.

So, it wasn't a huge adjustment when Cornell returned for kindergarten. This brought on a new set of concerns for us. Would he be able to hack it in a mainstream classroom? Would the other students react to him favorably? If he fell behind, would he become frustrated? Give up? I'd never seen Cornell give up, but every kid has his limits; right?

His teacher was a young, optimistic, and spirited woman who put in the extra effort to make sure Cornell stayed alongside his classmates as much as possible. We had more concerns than we could admit, but this teacher brought us back to believing again. Yes, Cornell was learning at a slower pace than the others, but he was grasping all the concepts with some extra time and effort, and we knew Cornell had no problem with extra effort.

We left that first parent-teacher conference arm in arm, full of relief and euphoria. *Look how far our little boy has come.* To think back to where he'd started and be told now that he would continue to be mainstreamed through elementary school was extraordinary.

Fall became winter, then spring, and then a glorious summer. In Virginia, the air is still sticky and the breeze warm when it's time to head back to school. The photos we have of Cornell and Kaitlyn, sitting on the steps by our kitchen, backpacks secured, heading to specific first grades, and Kristen toddling around, are some of my favorites.

Cornell's teacher would be a long time, respected first grade teacher and we already knew a lot about her. She had a fantastic reputation in the community, so we really psyched Cornell up for meeting her.

On the second day of school, Mrs. S (we will call her that) called Kim at home. We were thrilled to hear from her so early. Kim answered the phone and waved me over.

"Mrs. S, so nice to hear from you." She smiled.

"Yes, well…" I could hear her speaking in short breaths. "I wish I was calling with good news. But…"

Kim's expression changed, and she stopped short with the phone.

"Cornell forgot to lock the bathroom door, and another student walked in on him. And he was on the computer and he locked it up. He is having a very difficult time following basic instructions."

Kim waited for more of the story, but apparently, we'd reached the climax of it already. "I'm sorry you had to deal with that," she humored the teacher. "I'll remind him of locking the door. As far as the computer, maybe we can do some things at home to help with whatever you all are working on."

To our dismay, it became obvious in the first week of school that Mrs. S had zero tolerance for Cornell and no desire to work with him. The differences between kindergarten and first grade were stark. At no point in Cornell's life had we taken the "let's wait and see what happens" attitude. The start of first grade was no exception. We organized a couple of meetings with Mrs. S, but she was awfully rigid in the way she would run her classroom. It wasn't like we were trying to change that, but Cornell would need some level of flexibility from her in order to be successful. We knew there were going to be challenges. We knew accommodations would need to be made for him to learn. We thought the school knew that too. Apparently not.

This back and forth continued for 6 weeks before our confrontations escalated to the leadership at the school. We were met with a cold, hard wall from the leadership of the school. It was clear that the elementary school we had so much confidence in, had no interest in helping our son. At least in the manner we thought.

It baffled me at the time. I would look at my son and think, who wouldn't want him in their classroom? The only conclusion I could come to was that the school was concerned about their Standard of Learning test scores. If Cornell was kept in regular classes, he would take the same standardized tests the other students took and not score nearly as high on them. Hence, they wanted Cornell in the special ed class. He was in a tough spot: from our perspective he was functioning too high to be placed full time in special ed classes, but definitely slower to learn than the regular kids.

How could two teachers, in the same school, have such vastly different philosophies? We'd been so amped up after the previous year, but now we were spiraling downward. Regardless, it seemed no one was in Cornell's corner, and everyone was determined to remove him from first grade.

There was no point in trying to put a square peg in a round hole. It was time to explore other options. I'd heard about a place called

Chesapeake Bay Academy that specialized in students who just didn't fit in traditional classrooms for one reason or another. When we toured the school, we noticed some kids were learning disabled, some were in the genius range, and some dealt with social obstacles. It was fascinating and encouraging, the way they could all be in one room, challenged and learning. There were only ten students to a classroom with both a teacher and an aid. Each child was on their own customized learning track. Parental involvement and homework would be an absolute. Every teacher we met emphasized his or her desire to extract the very best from each student. It was an expensive private school but seemed a perfect fit for Cornell. In fairness, there was no way the neighborhood elementary school could compete, with what our son needed. When we met the principal, we immediately enrolled him.

We let his previous school know we were officially leaving, and they were shocked. I almost chuckled about it. What did they expect us to do? Stay in a place that didn't have faith in my son?

"It seems awfully optimistic that Cornell will be capable of reading and writing," they told us.

"My wife and I believe you're underestimating his potential. You have no idea what he is capable of. No one does. But we are going to find out. It's just not going to happen here." I said, and that was that. Kim and I had seen Cornell in the same light for years now. We knew that he was not scratching the surface of what was possible.

Shortly after our departure, Cornell needed another procedure at The Children's Hospital. The doctors wanted to check out his surgical site internally, which involved outpatient general anesthesia and a bronchoscope put down his throat. Compared to procedures he'd had in the past, this was nothing.

We could hardly believe it when a great big get-well card arrived from Mrs. S and her first-grade students. It was colored with all types of crayons and would have been taken as a nice gesture, if Mrs. S hadn't been held in such disregard in our household. Maybe she was feeling guilty. Who knows? In hindsight it was a really nice gesture. But Kim and I were still angry.

Cornell's recovery was quick, and he went on to Chesapeake Bay Academy. He thrived there, particularly with his new teacher. She used creative strategies to help him learn and provided us with a ton of feedback. She wouldn't just let us know his progress, but she'd also give us ways to facilitate his learning at home. With a little bit of time and effort, Cornell's reading and writing became a reality. Did he learn at the same pace as everyone else? No, he didn't. Does that matter? No, it doesn't. While many people would be bothered by this, Cornell had let that ship sail a long time ago. The fact that he could learn at his own pace, what he would later describe as "Cornell Time," was a perfect fit for him.

Every child at CBA was pushed to the limit academically, and every person was celebrated for being an individual with amazing gifts to offer. With each passing day, Cornell's self-esteem grew (if that were possible). It cost us a small fortune to send him to the academy but was worth every cent. At times, I wondered what would have happened if we didn't have the means to send Cornell to this amazing place. How many people exist in this world that simply don't fit the "normal" educational timetable and don't get their chance? It hurts deep within to think his spirit may have been squashed.

One school night, we'd finished dinner, the dishes, and the like, and sat down to do an activity with Cornell. Kim suggested he write a thank you card to his previous first grade class. I couldn't help but chortle. I knew what Kim was doing. Only part of her wanted to actually thank the class, while most of her wanted to make sure the teachers were aware our son was writing.

He spent time on it, and the next day, Kim drove over to his previous school to drop it off. The secretary took the envelope and stuck it into the first grade's mailbox. Just outside the office, my wife bumped into one of the parents she knew.

"Kim! I hear there is change afoot. How's Cornell doing?"

"It is early, but I think it is what we needed to do. He is thriving."

As the conversation continued with her friend, the aide from Mrs. S's class walked into the office to grab the mail, not acknowledging them. Kim heard the *rip, rip, rip* sound of the envelope; then the aide's retreating footsteps on the linoleum stopped. She turned to face Kim.

There wasn't a "hello" or anything of that nature. Instead, the woman looked at Kim, with her mouth agape, and demanded, "Did he write this?"

"Yep!" Kim smiled, and strutted out of the school.

I would have given almost anything to be there that day. I rarely get to see Kim strut.

—⁂—

Early in the kids' elementary years, Kim's best friend Shannon moved into our house with her four kids for a few weeks. They were caught between selling a house and having their next house ready. It was a little chaotic, but we were able to put a roof over their heads. Shannon had three boys, all around Cornell's age, and the youngest was a girl. Cornell loved those boys. Grayson and Cameron were the oldest and treated Cornell like any other friend of theirs. They ran hard, played hard, and cut Cornell no slack—not that he wanted it.

Around this time, Kim had been elbowing me to teach Cornell to ride a bike. Honestly, I was dreading it. I wasn't convinced he had the coordination to master riding a bike, and the last thing I wanted to do was see him hurt. I kept telling Kim I would teach him and purposely putting it off. When would I learn to stop underestimating my son?

I'll do my best to tell you this story as it was told to me by extremely excited young boys. Apparently, Grayson and Cameron took Cornell out into the front yard and told him they'd teach him to ride a bike. Cornell would have done anything those guys wanted, so he most likely shrugged his shoulders and said okay, with a big smile on his face.

They pushed him around the yard, and every time they let go, Cornell crashed into trees, a fence, the cement, you name it. And yet, the boys kept encouraging him, and Cornell kept hopping back on the bike. I don't know how long it took, but by the time I arrived home, my son was euphoric and showed me his brand-new skill set.

All of us were thrilled. Well, everyone except Kaitlyn, who crossed her arms and glared at Cornell like he'd just taken the head off her favorite doll. She set her jaw, picked up her own bike, and huffed, "Come on Dad! You need to teach me!" She didn't even look in my direction when she said it. I figured I'd better hop to.

Forty-five minutes later, my determined "twins" were both bike riders, with a slew of Band-Aids to prove it.

This time, Cornell had pushed Kaitlyn.

7

IRON DREAMS REALIZED

By now, Cornell was rubbing off on me. I had started applying myself more fully, and I had seen the effect it was having on my practice and our lifestyle. My son also grounded me in a way that is difficult to describe. At work, I wanted to do my dentistry as well and as efficiently as possible, so I could be a present dad/husband afterward. I was trying to balance my time as much as I could. What had suffered through all this was my general health. I had not exercised a lick, and I'd gained a lot of weight. I was ready to use some of Cornell's principles to achieve a big goal and get my health back.

During my years in college and dental school, I'd competed in many triathlons and road races. I know that not everyone shares in this sensation, but there's no feeling like pushing your body to its limits. When I ran, or biked, or swam to the point where I reached that high—that feeling of euphoria—the rest of my day was balanced in a way it couldn't have been otherwise. I missed that feeling.

The first time I saw the Hawaiian Ironman Triathlon was on TV in 1982. I was mesmerized. Those athletes completed a 2.4-mile swim, 112-mile bike ride, and 26.2-mile run in one day. I was captivated by the seeming impossibility of such a feat. Julie Moss, who had been leading the race, completely ran out of gas only a hundred yards from the finish line. In one of the most memorable moments in Ironman history, after collapsing several times, she literally crawled to the finish line, only to be passed by her second place tailer. Both of them were phenomenal. Talk about pushing your body to the limit!

Years passed, but somewhere in the back of my mind, I still thought about the Ironman. As I approached forty, I realized I'd put on about thirty pounds since my dental school days. I was considerably out of shape. My son's ability to always give 100 percent was also tapping me on the shoulder. What could I accomplish with such effort? I couldn't shake the feeling that exploring the boundaries of what is possible would be beneficial.

I put together a two-year plan that would conclude in the completion of an Ironman. It would involve running first. Short distances initially. Purchasing a bike at some point, and then eventually getting back in the pool.

When I told my family, the kids were excited; but I could see that Kim, while happy for my getting healthy, was concerned about the time involved. Regardless, the goal was made, and we would figure it out. Kim bought in. Which meant it was time to go to work.

I was really out of shape, so my first race would be a slow 5K, just to get my body back into moving like that again. I would need to start very slow. I felt a little like a fish out of water putting on my new running gear and lacing up the shoes I'd had custom-fitted to my feet. After a few weeks of running every day, someone showed up and wanted to help.

"Hey, Dad," Cornell said, watching me lace up my second shoe.

"Hey, buddy."

"Going running?" he asked.

"Yep."

"Can I come?"

I stopped looping and looked up at his inquisitive face. "You want to run with me?"

How would this work? I certainly didn't want to say no to such an innocent request, but I wasn't sure Cornell would have the wherewithal to run two to three miles.

As I pep-talked myself into not doubting his ability, he interrupted my thoughts, saying, "I'll ride my bike."

That was a much easier pill to swallow. Cornell was becoming a great bike rider, and I knew he'd be just fine by my side. He was off to the garage for his helmet and bike. We were out and about for almost a half hour, but it felt like a much shorter amount of time with Cornell along. He told me stories, commented on the clouds in the sky, waved at our neighbors, and oozed the positive energy that embodied his spirit.

"Hey, thanks for keeping me company," I told him when we returned to the driveway.

"Sure, Dad. I'll go with you next time, too, if you want," he assured me, wheeling his bike back into the garage.

"I'd like that."

All my focus went toward running first. My goal was to complete a marathon before I started in on the swimming and biking. Every time I went out running, Cornell was by my side with his bike. Occasionally, Kaitlyn would join us as well.

I'd heard about a group that met at Final Kick Sports on Saturday mornings, for long runs. I knew I was in serious need of someone to help me with this endeavor, so when I met the owner of this establishment, Jerry Frostick, I knew I had found my coach. He was instrumental in laying out the plan that would allow me to reach my goal.

When I finally could run eight miles, I attempted to run with the Saturday-morning group at Final Kick, but it wasn't the same. There was something about running with Cornell by my side. Number one, he liked to run his mouth the entire time. It was like having a motivational trainer with me every step of the way. Second, when I would struggle and probably have a look of absolute pain on my face, Cornell's expression was that of optimism. He would squash the *I'll never make it* thoughts from my head and say things like, "We're almost to the next mile," or, "I'm good. You good, Dad?"—and I'd pull myself to a place so I could answer, "Yes, I'm good." He loved being a part of this journey with me and almost literally pulled me along.

At the end of our eight-mile loop, I introduced myself to the pacers.

"Hey, John, glad to have you in the group," Jerry said.

"Listen, I have an unorthodox question."

Jerry folded his arms across his chest. He was interested in whatever I was bringing to the table.

"My son, Cornell, he always rides his bike alongside me when I run. He's only eight, but he's kind of my motivator."

"Wow, that's awesome."

"So, I'm wondering if he could join this Saturday's running group on his bike. We won't get in the way. The two of us can hang behind; we'll be the caboose. What do you think?"

"Sounds good to me," he said, and others who had gathered nodded in agreement.

We did the shorter runs together from the house during the week, while on Saturdays we'd drive forty minutes to Virginia Beach, where we'd fall into pace, behind one of the many Final Kick groups headed out.

Cornell always came with me.

One weekend, as we worked towards the marathon distance, my training schedule called for a twenty-mile run on Saturday. My alarm went off that February morning, and I heard the wind slam against the side of the house. The night before, the Weather Channel had predicted it would be about 25 degrees all day. My run was set to go through Sea Shore State Park—to the end of the boardwalk in Virginia Beach and back. A long ten miles out and ten miles back. I started looking for excuses immediately, but when I walked out of my bedroom to drink a cup of coffee, Cornell was sitting on the couch, fully clothed and tying his shoes. We were doing this.

I made sure each of us had the right jacket, hat, gloves, socks and such to keep us as warm as possible. We wore layer upon layer. I have to admit, part of me was nervous. I didn't know how I was going to complete such a distance in these weather conditions, let alone how my eight-year-old son was going to fare. But Cornell acted like he didn't notice or care about the icy weather. He hopped in the car the same way he would if it were sixty-five and sunny.

"You ready?" I asked him when we got there.

"Are *you* ready, Dad?" he asked, and all I did was smile, because I didn't have an answer.

We made the drive to the beach and parked the car. We zipped up and set out. The wind was at our backs going out those first ten miles, which meant, well, need I tell you what the wind was like on the way back? The wind was blistering, stinging, devastating, thrashing—pick your adjective. It was absolutely kick-in-the-teeth miserable. Parts of me were sweating while other parts were freezing.

I mustered up the energy to turn my head toward Cornell. There was my son, with a history of breathing issues, leaning into the wind, coming directly off of the Atlantic Ocean, and grinding it out. From about mile ten to fourteen, we were along the boardwalk with no cover from the trees, moving into "the teeth of it." It was a tough stretch all around. Cornell and I didn't talk much during those miles, maybe a grunt here and there, but he did not complain once. I wanted to stop, walk, quit, and go find a cup of hot coffee. But Cornell… he had to be suffering twice as much as I, and I didn't see one moment of hesitation or even second-guessing. He'd set a goal for us, and that was that.

When we crossed our designated twenty-mile finish line, the two of us were in a bit of a daze for a few minutes. Were we really finished?

We'd kept such perpetual motion our bodies felt awkward putting a halt to it.

In the parking lot, we hugged and high-fived, and as we climbed back into the car, Jerry came running out.

"Are you guys *nuts?*" he said. "Seriously dude, that is *awesome.* You have no idea what completing a run like that will do for you on race day."

"Nice job, Dad." Cornell sported his famous grin and looked at me. He had ice in his eyebrows.

"Come here," I said, picking out the shards. It felt like just last week that we had celebrated his ability to walk. He'd propelled himself so far in such a short amount of time.

During the dark hours of training in the next year, I would replay this training session in my head. In fact, anytime I was faced with something I didn't want to do, I remembered that day.

Soon my training schedule included swimming, biking, and running. In preparation, I ran multiple 5Ks, 10Ks, half marathons, The Vegas Marathon, and multiple short-course triathlons. I also did two half Ironmans (1.2-mile swim, 56-mile bike, and 13.1-mile run). Through it all, when I was running, Cornell on his bike, was my training buddy.

On November 9, 2002, I competed in the Florida Ironman. What I forgot to tell Cornell is that I wouldn't actually be in contention. The pro athletes finish these races in under nine hours. This race was no exception. I had told Cornell that he had earned the right to run the last quarter mile with me, but when he saw the pro finish, he was expecting to see me right behind him. Kim tried to explain that I was hours away from finishing (I was literally just starting my marathon when the pros finished), but Cornell was not having any of it. He stood in the same spot, a quarter mile from the finish line, and waited for me for *six hours.*

The Ironman is unlike any other sporting event. You might expect that only highly competitive, elite athletes compete. But the reality is, of the 1,800 competitors that hit the water at seven A.M., probably only 300 to 400 are there to win at an age group or professional level. The other 1,400 are there for all sorts of reasons. Some began as a big, hairy, audacious goal (Good to Great, Jim Collins 2001) to lose weight; others to learn about themselves; some as a fundraiser; and for others, the reason is so personal we will never know. But because of this, it is one of the most positive events on earth. Eighteen hundred people, all hitting the water at the same time, with seventeen hours to finish the task. They all cover 140.6 miles, spread out between a swim, a bike ride, and a run. And as each competitor finishes, they wait, to celebrate the other finishers, until the cut off time of midnight.

As you can imagine, there are some highs during the day, but there are a lot of lows, which really challenge the inner workings of your own belief system, of what you think is possible.

I can remember how beat I was feeling at mile 20 of the run. It was dark, I was alone, and six more miles seemed like an eternity. But, like I had done other times during the day, my thoughts turned to Cornell, and the night I saw him choose life. He was all in, so I kept putting one foot in front of the other.

As badly as I felt at mile 20, it's hard to describe the feeling of finally hearing the noise from the finish line, off in the distance. Music blaring, the crowd cheering, and then, as I turned the final corner, a quarter mile out, there was Cornell, standing in his spot with my family. Tears began streaming down my face.

As I ran by him, he matched my shuffle, side by side. We entered the finishing chute, which is about twenty feet wide and one-eighth mile from the finish line. Bleachers filled with people screaming for the athletes, while the huge speakers blasted Cher's hit song *Believe*, making the hairs on my neck stand straight up on end.

The emcee screamed over the mic, "John Cranham! You are an Ironman!"

Inexplicably, I felt no pain. We sprinted the last fifty yards to the finish line.

I had hit the water at 7:00 A.M. and crossed the finished line at 9:50 P.M., fourteen hours and fifty minutes later. No records were set, but man, did I feel incredible! I had taped a picture of Cornell, when he was younger with his trach, to the handlebars of my bike. With his help, I explored my limits and completed something that I did not think possible. I'm confident I wouldn't have attempted the Ironman, and certainly wouldn't have finished, if it hadn't been for my son. Most important, this experience stretched me, narrowing the gap between dreams and possibilities. It prepared me for things to come.

8

THE MAYOR

By the time Cornell reached the age of ten, his deficits for learning had become more noticeable. Kaitlyn and Kristen excelled beyond him effortlessly. Math, abstract reasoning, and the like were increasingly difficult for him. It became clear that mastering situations where abstract thinking was required was probably never going to happen… although I didn't like to use the word "never" with Cornell.

I bring this up because of an old friend of ours, whom I'll call Cindy. Cindy and her husband grew close to Kim and me, and then our families intertwined in one way or another. One weekend night, Kim and I were out to dinner with Cindy and her husband. We were having a nice time, talking about who knows what, when Cindy blurted out, "What are you guys doing to do with Cornell?" She sipped her wine. "He hasn't got a clue!"

I've never come so close to slapping a woman in all my life.

How a person, particularly someone we call a friend, have so little empathy to say that to a parent, bewilders me to this day.

Believe it or not, I could extract some good from this awful situation. What Cindy said is a good example of prejudice about disability. Our society, and how we view our kids revolves around learning objectives and—sometimes insane—standardized tests. She was comparing Cornell to the norm; and, yes, he was behind. Why wouldn't he be? But to say to another parent, that your child "doesn't have a clue", well that is still beyond my level of understanding.

It's been interesting to discover that some of the smartest, most educated people we know, both friends and family, are also the most judgmental. So many assume that because Cornell was caught by our country's safety net, he would never be able to rise out of it. There's this perception that the "gifted" are bound to be happier and more successful. They're the difference makers who are more important and, therefore, on a higher plane than those not on "their level."

Cornell made me realize that people feel happy and whole from a place within them that has nothing to do with money, IQ, or place in society. Cornell's life experience gave him emotional intelligence and a depth, that far superseded, many of the people pitying him. People who are genuinely happy, have enough. Enough to be independent, the capacity to take care of themselves, and some place to go to make a difference and feel valued. These were the goals we were continuing to strive toward—with all our kids.

—∞—

Chesapeake Bay Academy switched to a college-prep format for middle school and high school. We had a meeting with Cornell's teachers, who assured us he was doing well, but would be better served with the resources in the public school, moving forward.

After our experience with first grade, we were concerned about how Cornell and the public-school system would mix. He'd built up a phenomenal level of confidence at Chesapeake Bay, and we worried that a public middle school would tear all of it down.

Kim and I lay in bed that night with dramatic sighs between us. "His little spirit is so strong," Kim said. "But…" Her voice trailed off.

"I know. Do you think he'll be bullied?" I asked, pulling *Dentistry Today* from my nightstand.

Kim had rolled on her side, with her hands under her head as though praying. "Or he could be lost."

"Maybe we'll be wrong. He's surprised us a few times in the past." I put the pages down and looked at her. It was a funny thing for me to be the one telling Kim that our son might beat the odds after all, instead of the other way around.

"That he has." She smiled and rolled on her back, hands above her head. "He's also so small. Don't you think that will cause issues?"

"Kids are all sorts of shapes and sizes in middle school. That shouldn't be a problem." Or so I hoped.

We were about to say goodnight when I had a thought. "Do you think he could play in the middle school orchestra?" Cornell had been taking violin lessons now for five years and had been working very hard at it.

"He most certainly could," Kim assured me, turning out the light on her side of the bed. "Let's tell him tomorrow after work," she mumbled.

The following night, after dinner, we lingered around the table and told Cornell about his new school. While there was no outward response of negativity, he was a little quieter than normal.

"I know it's sad," Kim managed. "We've all loved Chesapeake Bay."

I chimed in., "But you know, your mom and I were thinking." Cornell kept his gaze on the table in front of him. "You might be able to play in the middle school orchestra."

You'd have thought the ceiling of our house had opened up and a sparkling light had come shining through onto Cornell's seat. He immediately perked up as if to say, *Tell me more.*

"As far as I can tell, it's a big orchestra, with concerts and such a few times a year."

"You mean I could play my violin with a bunch of other people?" he whispered.

In the blink of an eye, Cornell went off to middle school. The plan was for him to be placed in the special education/learning disability classes, with the opportunity to be mainstreamed for gym and orchestra. Cornell came home happy each day that first week, and then the second. However, every time we asked if he had homework, his response was always the same. "Not today."

One of two things was happening here: either Cornell wasn't being pushed, or he wasn't being honest. Neither Kim nor I remembered a time when Cornell had lied, so we called his teachers. They reiterated what our son had: the students were not being given homework.

"Would it be weird if I asked them to give him homework?" Kim questioned.

"Not sure. Would they throw him busy work?"

"Ugh. He's not going to be challenged like he was at Chesapeake Bay, is he?"

"Let's just give it some more time."

Once again, Cornell was stuck between the more involved special needs kids and the "normal" ones.

We did, indeed, ask Cornell's teachers to send work home with him. We believed homework was good practice and helped Cornell improve during "off hours." He liked coming home and completing homework along with his sisters, so it wasn't like we were putting him through some sort of painful exercise. After those initial few weeks, Kim and I said we were going to be hands-off and allow Cornell to find his niche in his new school, without his parents' involvement. Kim and I knew we could reach out whenever necessary. But we wanted to exercise some faith that all was well, and that Cornell was holding his own.

Sometime that fall, our family was at the mall. I can't recall what we were looking for, if anything, really. Sometimes it was fun to wander and stare at the store windows, with a stop at the food court.

Each of us were nibbling an Auntie Anne's pretzel when a cute young girl with bright blond hair passed by and waved. "Hi, Cornell," she said. She and her friend smiled like they had mustered up the courage to say hello to Brad Pitt.

"Hi," he responded, with a brief up and down of his hand.

Kim and I looked at Cornell. Kristen and Kaitlyn looked at Cornell. Cornell looked at his pretzel. Eventually, he noticed all of us staring at him.

"What?" he asked, with a sheepish grin on his face.

Kaitlyn asked the question we all had burning our tongues. "Who was that?"

Cornell shrugged. "I don't know. Someone from school?"

"Seemed like she knew you," Kim prodded, but Cornell only lifted his shoulders once again, not letting on how he really felt.

After that, we noticed Cornell's walk had gained… well, actually, to steal from his vocabulary, it had gained some swag. Cornell developed a bounce to his step that was all his own. Head up, eyes forward, walking (bouncing) with purpose. It was impossible to watch and not smile. It seemed the mall wasn't the only place he was noticed. Kids of all shapes and sizes would make sure to say hello to him at church, restaurants, and just about anywhere we went.

I received a phone call at my office from the gym teacher one afternoon. A phone call like this, at my office, midday, had never occurred before. Puzzled, I answered.

"Jeff Russell here. I wanted to take a second to share with you a little about Cornell in my class."

"Okay," I said, but still couldn't piece this together. Had Cornell done something? Had someone done something to him?

"Anytime we have basketball scrimmages in my class, Cornell is always, without fail, giving 100 percent effort. Not only that, but at his size, he's fearless about shooting the ball over kids twice his size. It's pretty impressive!"

I relaxed and chuckled slightly. "That sounds like Cornell."

"So, I won't take up more of your time, but I wanted to congratulate you on the leader your son is becoming, in my class, in particular."

I could hardly spit out a *thank you, goodbye* because tears were streaming down my cheeks. Mr. Russell noticed Cornell's heart, which was more important to me than anything else.

As an aside, we kept in touch with Jeff for a number of years and would occasionally play golf with him. He told us story after story of how Cornell carved his way into the hearts of the teachers. He'd been assigned to pick up the attendance sheet from the teacher in every classroom at the start of each day. He'd make sure to smile and greet everyone sincerely every morning. To this day, I wonder if they asked him to do that for the simple reason that it injected a positive vibe into the school on a daily basis. In the Teacher's lounge, he was referred to as "The Mayor." Cornell had the gift of drawing people in and getting them to pull for him.

We watched and waited for a change during that critical time as he started public school. Kim and I remembered our own middle school experiences—we were a mess! We did our best to prepare for a downward spiral in Cornell's confidence. We anticipated some long conversations about life not being fair, but none of that ever came to fruition. In spite of the fact that he couldn't do many of the things the other kids were doing, and that Kaitlyn was now learning material he couldn't begin to understand, Cornell continued to focus on his strengths. What *could* he do? He would do those things to the best of his ability. Cornell continued to improve and develop. Slowly, gradually, he made progress... the Cornell Way.

—◊◊—

Cornell's orchestra teacher was exactly what we hoped she would be: positive, patient, and encouraging. Quite a few of the students were more talented than he was, but it made no difference in his ability to participate. He was wholeheartedly accepted.

And then his teacher called.

"Cornell's been acting up in class," she informed Kim.

"I'm terribly sorry," Kim responded, albeit confused. "What's going on?"

"He has the music for the first violin, but he continues to play the music for the second violin," his teacher huffed.

It was a good thing Kim was the one called and not me. She was able to quickly decipher the actual issue. Cornell wasn't acting up at all. By now we knew Cornell had a very good ear. He'd learned to read music, but most of his learning was from hearing a piece and playing it afterward.

"Where, exactly, is he sitting?" Kim asked.

"I don't know why that matters," the teacher responded.

"Just humor me a minute; how close is Cornell sitting to the first violins?"

She thought for a minute, and said "Actually, he is sitting right next to them."

Kim smiled. "I think he is having a hard time blocking out the first violin section and is playing it by ear. Could you move him to the middle of the second violins? I promise, he is not trying to misbehave."

Our son was moved to the center of the second violins and, boom, problem solved. No more phone calls.

Cornell maintained a positive relationship with the music department. He loved being a part of such a group. We kept up his private violin classes at a local music store each week, to provide him extra help with the pieces so he would be prepared. Just like when he was younger, if asked to practice thirty minutes, Cornell would need to practice for ninety, and would do it gladly. He enjoyed it, and he knew it would take extra effort for him to keep up with the others. I marveled at his discipline.

And just like that, middle school came to an end. For "Corndog," a glorious time was over. Could rough waters be ahead?

9

LIVING STRONG

When Tiger Woods went on his pro golf rampage in the late nineties and early 2000s, Cornell and I were right there with him. To this day, we love watching him play. My son had loved golf since he could stand, and when he grew a little older, I'd take him to the driving range. Soon enough, Cornell and I were fitting in a quick nine after work. Kaitlyn often joined us when the kids were younger, but her interests stemmed elsewhere over time.

Some of our best father-son conversations took place while walking the fairways together. We would talk about school, the music he liked to listen to, girls, his sisters—everything. It was a way for me to see what he was thinking. I sometimes wondered if he really loved the game that much, or simply valued having that kind of time with me.

Cornell and I set out one late afternoon to play a few holes. He was in the last few months of his eighth-grade years, so we had plenty of reflecting to do:

Remember the time you…?

How about that one day when…?

When you were in eighth grade, did you…?

Are you sad to leave, or ready to go?

As we walked back to the locker room to change our shoes and grab a Coke before leaving, I heard Cornell wheezing slightly and then he put his hand to his chest. I observed him before saying anything. He didn't look panicked or upset but kept trudging along.

"You okay, son?"

"Just, hard to breathe right now. But I'm good."

Kim and I scheduled a routine checkup after that mild incident, with Cornell's brilliant surgeon who had performed the previous surgeries.

Dr. D reported back to us. "Now, a normal trachea is the size of a standard drinking straw. But where we did the surgery is now the size of a cocktail straw. Cornell's trachea is the shape of an hourglass. The air just can't get through the constricted area. It doesn't take much of a change in the diameter, even in one small area, to dramatically inhibit air flow. In fact, the size of diameter is inversely proportional to airway resistance by the power of four."

I ran some mental calculations. "So, if my math is right, are you saying that if the lumen of his trachea is cut in half, the airway resistance is sixteen times worse?"

"Yes. that is correct. And that narrow portion is much smaller than half the size of his normal trachea. I honestly don't know how he is doing what he is doing. But it may explain why he has grown so little. The body will not develop when it can't properly oxygenate."

"What do we do about it"? Kim asked.

"The only way to solve such a problem is to resect the part of the trachea that is narrow and sew the good ends together. I suppose I'm making this sound simple, but that's not the case. I will need to cut through all the scar tissue in the previous surgical sites, which means coming dangerously close to his vocal cords, numerous arteries, nerves, and veins."

"Jesus," I managed to mutter. "When is this kid going to get a break? He is doing so damn well."

I was beyond frustrated.

Dr. D continued. "If the surgery isn't done, Cornell's life will be at risk. However, undergoing the procedure also poses many risks, one of which will be leaving him unable to speak. Cornell is adult enough to be a part of the conversation, so my suggestion is that you sit down and talk to him about it. I want him all in, when we do this. The good news is, we have some time. This is not an acute situation."

"How much time?"

"I would like to do it inside of a year, max."

Kim and I drove home in silence. When our son got home from school that day, we sat down and explained the situation.

Kim said, "We'd like to make this decision together. Let us know when you think you are ready."

It was a lot for him to take in. Most eighth-grade students were deciding where to attend high school or what classes to take. Cornell must have felt like the Little Mermaid, wondering how to live life without a voice. "I'm not sure yet."

"That's okay," we assured him. "We are here to talk about it whenever you want.

—◦—

Over the years, shifting from an 85-percenter and going all in had paid off. I had built a nice dental practice and begun doing educational seminars for other dentists. It started locally, then regionally, and now I was being asked to speak all over the world. I had a business trip scheduled to England and Ireland. Kim and I thought it would be fun to make a family trip out of it.

Off we went. From a historical standpoint, we landed in London at a terrible time: 7/7, the day of the 2005 bombings. We were on the Gatwick express, coming into the city. We were able to get to Victoria Station before everything came to a halt.

I did my best to remain calm, but it took us nearly two hours to get a cab to take us on to the hotel. I figured all my lectures would be cancelled the following day, but in typical British fashion, everyone showed up. I lectured in London the first Friday, and Dublin, Ireland, the next Friday. That gave us ample time to do some sightseeing in both countries in between.

When in Ireland, Cornell and I took the opportunity to play some of the beautifully lush Irish courses. The golf courses are indescribable. The rolling hills, the ocean in the distance, the greenest green I had ever seen… as well as roses the size of pumpkins, and the ever present, maddening wind that makes the sport all the more difficult.

During one of our rounds, we walked up a large hill to an elevated green. The more we walked, the harder it was for Cornell to breathe.

Finally, he grabbed my arm and said, "Stop."

I'd never known my son to slow down, quit, or break like this. He must have been hurting. I tried not to panic when I turned to see his face.

"All the time in the world," I said attempting to bring his heart rate down. "I'm right here."

After a few minutes, he was almost back to his normal pace. "I'm good," he said leaning into me. I held him close, both of us relieved. "Dad, I don't want to live like this anymore. I think I'm ready for that surgery."

"We'll get the ball rolling as soon as we're home," I said.

I waited for him to confide in me that he was scared or nervous, but nothing like that came from his mouth. Instead, Cornell said, "Let's finish the round."

―⚹―

Memorial Day weekend of 2006, Cornell underwent an eight-hour surgery. Kim and I were with him leading up to the surgery and got ourselves ready for what would follow. We were told being older and stronger, he would most likely do well during the procedure. But, during the postoperative phase of care, he was to be given morphine for the very first time. The nurses told us he might react strangely.

Once the procedure started, Kim and I joined the girls in the waiting room. We had geared ourselves up for a long day of waiting, and while all of us were optimistic, surgery always left a person open for risks.

A few times throughout, one of the doctors would come out to see us and let us know Cornell was doing great. No complications. These updates meant more than any of us could articulate.

When it was over, we could meet him in Recovery. All four of us paraded through the nursing station to a drugged up and sleeping Cornell. Soon enough, Cornell opened his eyes. He was still highly sedated and unable to speak, but he grabbed his mom's hand.

"Hi, honey," Kim said to him afterward. "You're so brave." I could tell she was holding back tears. Cornell pointed to the yellow Livestrong bracelet Kim was wearing. "Are you living strong?" she asked, a question that sailed through our house often.

Cornell nodded, then drifted off.

He knew we were worried about him. In typical Cornell fashion, he was more concerned about our well-being, even though he'd just undergone an eight-hour procedure. He was always thinking of us before himself.

As the post-op hours went on, they amped up his levels of the opiate. Under the morphine, Cornell grew angry. Not in a vicious sort of way, but in a form that didn't jibe with the Cornell we knew. I suppose he reminded me of a grumpy, old man who didn't want anyone on his lawn. I shot Kim a look, like, *what's happening?* But the doctors told us we had nothing to worry about; people react all sorts of ways to morphine.

The drugs finally left the system, and we spent the rest of the Memorial Day weekend inside of Children's Hospital. The most important post-operative instruction was that he could not put tension on his trachea. It was a bit shorter now, so tipping his head backward could strain the trachea and cause it to tear apart—which would prove to be fatal. So, they tied a long suture from under his chin to his chest, to keep his chin pointed downward. They also kept him in the hospital a few more days.

There was Cornell walking around, head pointed towards the ground. The muscles in his shoulders and neck had to be sore. Kim would give him massages, and the area was super tight. But in typical Cornell form, he found the silver lining.

"Look, Dad. I am in the perfect position to play my new handheld video game!" And he pecked away on the device.

As the time went on, Cornell didn't lose his speech, but we knew almost immediately that his voice was going to be different. His vocal cords now produced a low, scratchy sound, and all of us, Cornell included, needed a little time to adjust to it. He also struggled to project his voice over any sort of crowd noise; a small price to pay, given what the alternative could have been.

By the end of the summer—Labor Day, to be exact—Cornell was tubing and wakeboarding full speed at the lake. While his voice never fully recovered, his breathing was completely normal, and silent, for the first time in his life. There was a noticeable increase in his stamina. We were over a massive hump.

10

STEPPING UP FOR ADDYSON

By the time Cornell was fourteen, our extended family had grown. My biological brother and sister never had children, but Kim's brothers were both married, with families. David and his wife, Sarah, had three children: Catherine, Emme, and Patrick. Brian and his wife, Amy, had two girls, Campbell and Addyson.

Addy was the last of that generation, born a year after the time of Cornell's surgery. She was a beautiful baby girl, and all of us were in celebration mode. But another shock awaited us.

A relatively new blood test was used at the time of her birth to look for various genetic diseases. Kim received a phone call from Brian that Addyson had tested positive for cystic fibrosis.

She hung up the phone. "What do you know about cystic fibrosis?" she asked me.

"I certainly learned about it in Pathology. It's a genetic disease that affects the pulmonary and GI systems. If I remember right, the survival rate is not good."

"Let's read about it," she said, motioning to our computer.

"What's going on?"

"Apparently Addyson might have it."

My heart raced.

We researched and found that, at the time, cystic fibrosis was the most common fatal inherited disease in the U.S., with about a thousand newly diagnosed cases in children each year. There is no cure, and only half of all people with CF live to age thirty. The treatment is so expensive that most insurance plans fall short.

I sunk into the chair, and Kim's shoulders hunched over me. We were silent until Cornell bounced into the room.

"What's up with you guys?"

"Call your sisters to the kitchen table, will you?" I asked.

"Sure," he said.

We sat the kids down and explained what was going on with Addyson. Kristen was quiet, Kaitlyn's brow furrowed, and it appeared Cornell made an inventory of questions in his head. Kim and I admitted we would be learning right along with them but would do our best to find answers to their questions.

Brian and Amy both had good jobs. Brian was in management and sales, and Amy worked for an ophthalmologist. But they didn't have the cash flow or the savings for what was coming. Kim and I realized they'd need to pay for medications, enzymes, and chest physical therapy, all of which could add up to thousands of dollars. We were not the type of family to shut off the computer and say, "Glad that's not me," before hitting the pillow.

Kim and I tossed around ideas to raise funds for baby Addy. David suggested an annual golf tournament, which would be great over time, but would not inject the family with the desperately needed immediate funds. We stewed. We worried. We kept thinking.

A little later on, and I'm vague because the days were incredibly difficult to keep track of when time was so precious, the kids and I sat down to dinner. We found ourselves in a deep discussion about the financial problems and what a fundraiser was.

"So, it's like a party where people buy stuff?" Kristen asked.

"People buy stuff, but all the money goes to help someone," Kaitlyn said.

Cornell said, "Do people have to buy stuff?"

Good question. I smiled at him. "Stuff? No. But people need to put money toward something. Remember when Relay for Life was going on a few years ago? People walked around the track and each time, they raised money. That money went toward helping people with cancer. Make sense?"

Later, Cornell approached me. "Dad? I have an idea."

"What's that?"

"I saw a kid on TV once shoot baskets, and he had something called 'sponsors.' Every time he made a basket, the sponsors gave him money."

"Do you want to shoot baskets for a fundraiser?"

"Dad, no." Cornell grinned at me like I was dense. "But I *can* hit a lot of golf balls."

I sat there, floored. Cornell had become somewhat of a legend at our golf club, wearing out the driving range. He loved to play golf, but he loved to hit balls even more. He would spend hours on the hottest day and not seem to wear out.

"That's true." I nodded.

"Maybe we could get sponsors and see how many golf balls I can hit in one day."

What more needed to be said? My heart started to race. By this time, I'd told Cornell's story hundreds of times from the podium. He was well known among some of the long-time employees at Children's Hospital of the King's Daughters. People would stand up for Cornell. They wanted to support him, and he was up to the task. Why not?

We called the event "Driving for a Cure," and scheduled it for August 30, 2007. A flyer was created and sent via email and snail mail to everyone we could possibly reach. Those who were interested could choose to be a Bronze, Silver, or Gold donor. Bronze donors wrote in a specific amount to pledge; silver donors gave fifty cents a ball, and gold donors would pay one dollar per ball.

The response was incredible. Before Cornell had set foot on the range, we'd raised *ten thousand dollars*. With the pledges from the silver and gold donors, Cornell would make 37 dollars every time he hit a ball into the grid.

With the idea in motion, Cornell spent hours on the range practicing during July and August. In the heat of the day, he would set up 250 to 300 balls and hone his swing. He got stronger, and developed calluses that would prove to be important. He was on a mission.

We worked with Cornell to set the parameters. A grid was set up at Cedar Point Country Club. Cornell would be given time from seven in the morning until seven at night to see how many full drives—as in, full swings with a driver—he could whack in one day. We agreed to set up one thousand golf balls at the start of the day. If he could go through those in twelve hours, then he'd make between twenty and thirty thousand dollars. All of us believed he could do it if he really pushed himself. As we looked at the forecast for the day of the event, it was going to be sunny and *hot*.

We all woke up early that beautiful Thursday morning. Cornell and I drove to the course around six-thirty, alone. Cornell's a great morning person, animated and talkative. However, that morning he was quiet, and his face was serious.

"What's on your mind?" I asked.

Cornell's demeanor was as grave as I had ever seen it.

He then asked, "How long will it take before I start to hurt?"

I laughed, but he shot me a look that let me know he wasn't joking. He was preparing to push himself to the limit and was dead serious. Today wasn't fun and games to Cornell.

"There will be pain today," I explained. "With every great effort, there is discomfort. Remember, we will be there the entire time to support you."

Cornell nodded. He was ready.

At seven A.M., it was just the five of us. Cornell stepped onto the tee box. He was only four-foot-nine and weighed 85 pounds. But he was lean and strong, like a taut wire. As every golfer knows, you never know who is going to show up on any given day—the good golfer, or the struggling golfer. Cornell's first drive soared 190 yards, with a slight draw, right down the middle of the range. As good as I had ever seen him hit it.

I turned to Kim and said with a smile, "This could be very interesting."

It became clear his back would go out quickly if he had to bend down to tee up every single ball. So, Kaitlyn and Kristen took turns teeing up the balls throughout the day. With his iPod in his back pocket, and ear buds in both ears and taped to the side of his face, Cornell found his rhythm. Drive after drive flew down the middle of the grid. By one o'clock, he'd burned through the first thousand balls we'd set out. Can you believe it?

He took a swim, ate lunch, put on his "Tiger Woods" outfit—black shorts and a blood red shirt—and got back to business.

The sun blazed, and we were joined by friends, family, and colleagues throughout the day. By now, Cornell was blistering and bleeding. One of us would tape him up, and he'd choose to go back to the tee. His pace slowed, but his contact remained pure.

The midafternoon heat lingered, and word had spread. More people showed up to witness Cornell's effort. Then a local TV station video crew. They shot video of him hitting and then asked for a brief interview. Cornell said sure and sauntered over to the pretty, young newswoman standing in front of the camera.

"I'm here with Cornell Cranham at his fundraiser, Driving for a Cure. Cornell, why are you hitting all these golf balls today?" She lowered the microphone.

Cornell, the little fella who would never walk or talk, who would never really be able to show affection to us, or love us, looked directly into the camera and in his own stammering words said, "When I was a little boy, lots of people helped me through it. So now, I am here for Addyson. Brian and Amy have always been a great uncle and aunt, and I know today is going to be hard for them. I just want to make today special for Addyson and all of the other people sick with CF." He politely thanked the crew for coming, flashed his million-dollar smile, and continued hitting balls.

A thought hit me at that moment: only one member of the entire family had any life experience with respiratory depression. Cornell had asked me some tough questions about Addyson including, specifically, what happens to kids with CF when they get sick, and how they die. We had explained that cardiorespiratory failure was the typical fatal culprit.

Our son was too young to recall most of the events he had lived through, but they still lived in his soul. His life experience was driving him. Cornell knew exactly why he was placed on this Earth that breezy, August day. I'd never seen such clarity of vision.

Just shy of seven P.M., blistered, bloody, and exhausted, Cornell sat down. He had just hit his 1,620th full drive into the grid.

He looked up at me and asked, "Dad, have I made a difference yet?"

I rushed over, gave him a hug, and said, "Yes, buddy. This has been *unbelievable!*"

After all the math was done, Cornell had raised just south of seventy thousand dollars for Cystic Fibrosis, and his cousin Addyson. *In. One. Day.*

That night, with my children soundly sleeping and my wife reading a book, I thought back thirteen years earlier, to the day we brought Cornell home. If you'd told me then that Brian and Amy would someday have a daughter with cystic fibrosis and that someone in the family would raise nearly seventy grand for her in one day, the last person on the list would have been Cornell. It would have seemed impossible in every form. And yet, it happened right before our eyes. I grinned and rolled over.

11

"MANAGING" HIS WAY THROUGH HIGH SCHOOL

Kaitlyn and Cornell went on to attend separate high schools. The biggest contrast was the size of the two schools. Kaitlyn's freshman class was around eighty students, while Cornell's was over five hundred. That meant two thousand kids walked the halls during a passing period! Not only that, but the sheer size of the adolescent students was a change, as well. Any number of the students towered over me, let alone Cornell, who had yet to reach five feet.

Cornell was still playing the violin, and I suppose we hadn't thought a lot about high school orchestra until we spoke with the woman who ran his middle school orchestra. Her husband conducted the high school ensemble, which meant she was familiar with the lay of the land over there. She was candid with Kim and me when we saw her.

"They expect the kids to be able to play highly complex pieces of music and learn their part at home. That way, they can focus on the nuances when they are together." She wasn't apologetic or pitying, and I appreciated that.

All Kim and I could say was, "Oh."

"Cornell was wonderful in the middle school orchestra, but he won't make it in high school," the music teacher said. "It's insanely competitive."

We were trying to figure out how we were going to tell Cornell that his orchestra days were coming to an end. Neither of us saw this coming. We said our goodbyes and walked away in silence. Kim and I knew we were thinking the same thing: how were we going to have this conversation with our son? Orchestra was such a big part of his middle school experience. Surely, he'd be devastated that he couldn't participate in high school.

We didn't drag our feet on the looming talk we needed to have. We called Cornell to sit at the kitchen table and point-blank told him he would not be able to play in the high school orchestra. We detailed what his old teacher told us, and said we were so sorry to report such news.

Cornell's disappointment showed, but we could see he was thinking rather than stewing. After only a few seconds, he asked, "Can I still take lessons at The Music Staff?"

"Absolutely."

"Do you think I could learn to play the guitar too? I mean they have people at the studio that teach guitar, right".

"Yes, I believe they do, and we can see about it."

"If I am taking my lessons, can I still play in the Christmas and year-end recitals they have?"

"Yes."

"Okay… I really liked playing with the middle school orchestra, but as long as I can still keep playing music, and get to be in Music Staff recitals, I am good with that."

And, so, on we went.

—⁓—

We kicked off the school year with a parent-teacher conference at Cornell's school. Surely, he would feel tiny. Certainly, he would feel lost in such a massive environment. Just like the start of middle school, we braced ourselves for a change in his attitude, his demeanor. We prepared for the other shoe that was about to drop.

Within the first few weeks, when we asked Cornell about school, he'd tell us about the adults there—coaches, teachers, security guards, the assistant principal, and so on. We knew he was once again caught in the middle, too high functioning for the Special Ed kids, but not quite able to keep up with the mainstreamed students. I was torn between believing he'd carve out his own path, as he'd done in the past, and waiting for him to be frustrated by his limitations.

One of the people Cornell mentioned often was a teacher the students called Moose. He was a husky, jovial guy, who was also the assistant coach of the varsity football team. Rarely did I see him when he wasn't sporting a school t-shirt, and he wore a perpetual grin on his face. Soon after we heard about Moose, Cornell came bouncing through the front door after school one day.

"I'm going to be the manager of the football team," he said, pouring himself some water from the faucet and whisking away, into the next room.

"That's great, honey," Kim said, not wanting to question this yet.

I don't know how it happened or whose idea it was, but sure enough, Cornell was detailing his responsibilities to us over dinner. He'd have to be at every practice possible and would stand with the team on the sidelines during games. He was responsible for making sure all the equipment was organized and in order, as well as anything related to keeping the players and coaches hydrated and healthy. He was incredibly amped up about his job.

"Isn't this awesome?" he asked, practically out of breath from all the information that had spewed out of him.

"We can come watch the games and see you doing your job," Kristen chimed in, clearly proud of such an idea.

"That would be great!" Cornell was already off in la-la land, imagining himself in his newly appointed position. "Kaitlyn, maybe you can come once in a while too?"

She'd been quiet most of dinner. "For sure." She looked up from her food just long enough to let Cornell know she was proud of him too.

"Cool." He leaned back in his chair like he had everything a guy could ever want. And maybe he did.

Friday-night football is a rite of passage for most high school students in Virginia. With cooler fall air comes intense, hard-hitting competition between rivals. Stands full of screaming fans, led by a host of enthusiastic cheerleaders, are all part of it. The Western Branch football team had good years and mediocre years when Cornell was there. They never won state or anything like that, but the school still carried a proud football culture. Friday-night games under the lights were an exhilarating experience, and our son was right in the middle of the action.

Cornell remained the manager of the team all four years of high school. His last home game as a senior stands out in my mind. Kim and I were there, bundled in coats and scarves, watching Western Branch get their butts kicked. They were down two or three touchdowns at half. The whip of the cold air and the sting of defeat at a final home game, were interchangeable.

When the halftime buzzer rang, the Western Branch football players slowly jogged off the field with their heads down, but Cornell wasn't among them. I spotted him midfield with a football, purposefully not following the team. I looked at Kim, and we both knew this was odd. The locker room at halftime was one of the places Cornell most loved to be during a game. We then saw the coach standing near the locker room, calling his name and motioning for him to join the team.

I cannot recall a time when Cornell wasn't respectful and obedient. He's always been a serious pleaser whose goal in life is to make other people happy. For him to not do as the coach requested, well… I wasn't sure what to make of it. Something was going on, though. Cornell kept shaking his head no to the coach. After his third attempt, the head coach ran out to meet him at midfield. They talked for a minute or two and then parted ways. Cornell went to sit on the bench about fifty feet in front of us, and the coach ran to the locker room.

Kim and I were at a loss. There wasn't much to do but wait until later, when we could ask him what was going on.

When the second half started, a different Western Branch football team took the field. Almost like superheroes, they scored twenty-one points and won the game in the final seconds. When the final buzzer sounded and the team was officially victorious, several of the players ran over to Cornell, gave him a high five, and slapped him on the back. Then they all ran him into the locker room.

If we were confused before, we were mystified now.

Later that night, when Cornell arrived home with an all-encompassing glow, Kim couldn't help herself. "What a game! What happened out there?"

But Cornell only shrugged. "They were awesome in that second half though. Right?"

Teenagers. Why can't they tell you everything you want to know?

We really didn't know what took place during that game until a few days later. The coach called my office with an explanation.

"When I tried to get Cornell to go into the locker room with us, he told me he didn't want to go. He said these guys had already quit, and it wasn't going to be any fun in there. He told me he would give anything to be big enough and strong enough to be able to play this game. He was upset that they were not even willing to try their hardest. Said that it was his last time as a manager, and he didn't want to see them all sad in the locker room. He asked if it was okay if he stayed outside. He didn't want it to end like this."

The coach did not tell me everything he said to the team that night, but he used Cornell's sentiments as fuel. He did say that he ended his speech with, "Boys, we should be ashamed of ourselves!"

The rest is history.

At the final awards banquet, the coach doled out high school letters to the players. He also had one for Cornell. When he introduced our son to the crowd, the coach said, "This next young man is why I do what I do."

—⟋⟍—

At the end of the football season during his sophomore year, Cornell was loving the ride of working with the team. He told us he was worried about having "nothing to do" when winter came. What I'm about to tell you makes me laugh every time I think of it, mainly because, like many things, we didn't hear the whole story until much later.

A few days after the football season ended, the athletic director of the school looked up from his desk to find Cornell sitting in the chair across from him. Somehow he'd got past his secretary and, unannounced, plopped himself in the chair in front of the man's large oak desk. Cornell had befriended him in the past, so it wasn't strange for them to talk, but inviting himself into his office was something different.

"Can I help you?" he said.

"I've been thinking. I did such a good job with the football team, maybe I could manage the basketball team."

The A.D.'s eyebrows went up. Cornell was magic.

Introductions were made to the head varsity basketball coach, and the plan was set in motion. He was taught to set up the video camera on the tripod and how to record all the games. Once again, he was at all practices and traveled with the team. The best part was watching Cornell—four-foot-ten and ninety pounds—high-five the tallest kids in school.

12

BIRACIAL CHALLENGES & KRISTEN'S PERSPECTIVE

After Kaitlyn was born, Kim and I bought a double stroller, the kind you'd push twins around in. When Kaitlyn was six months old, Cornell was two, and they were about the same size. Therefore, except for the color of their skin, they looked like twins.

Kim and I would often take the kids to the mall, just to be out and about. We'd roll them around in the stroller, with Kaitlyn up front and Cornell in the back, due to all of his equipment; we'd store most of it on the rack underneath. Babies draw attention anyhow, but double strollers really catch people's eyes. Mall passersby would light up, make faces, and say hello to Kaitlyn before making their way to the baby in the back. I wish I had video of all the ways people reacted.

Some laughed out loud in utter surprise. "Oh, my goodness, hello!"

Others looked exasperated, probably wondering, *how am I supposed to react to this?*" and quickly scurried away.

One African American girl put her hands on her hips, looked at Kim, and said, "Girrrrlll, how'd you do *that?*"

Our excursions became sociological studies. The numerous varied ways that people responded to our family was sometimes overwhelming.

We never knew what was coming. Some looked at us with great love and understanding, while others, quite clearly, viewed us with hate.

Over time, I came to realize prejudice crosses all racial lines. Whites and blacks seemed to love us or hate us equally. Some whites respected us for what we were doing, and others hated us for it. The exact same ratio seemed to exist in the black population.

Kaitlyn and Cornell could have cared less. For the first eight to ten years of Kaitlyn's and Cornell's lives, they were inseparable. They went in the same direction, shared the same interests, and were best friends. It wasn't complicated.

In no uncertain terms, Kim and I were naive about the potential challenges of bringing home a child like this. Although we'd spent months anticipating the medical challenges, the curve ball came in the way the world was going to view our family.

Kim and I were both brought up in homes that were not racist. I won't deny having biases that white families often had, but in no way did either one of us look at black people with any sort of negativity. We may have left the hospital with rose-colored glasses and an assumption that everyone would accept us, but that sentiment didn't last long.

Today, people talk an awful lot about white privilege—the invisible asset whites enjoy that nonwhites do not experience. The United States has a long way to go to create a level playing field for all Americans, regardless of skin color. Is there white privilege? Do white people have an edge over African Americans? There is no question. But, on the other side of that, can I, a white man, change the way I grew up? No, I cannot. I can, however, recognize this disparity and try to do something about it. We can all try to understand all sides of this issue and strive to make it better. Kim and I thought that bringing Cornell home could even be a small step forward. I suppose that's why I was so shocked when, days after bringing Cornell home, we received a phone call.

A woman's voice with a deep Southern drawl was on the other end. "Is this Mr. Cranham?"

"Yes," I answered. She told me her name, but I can't recall it.

"I'm calling to confirm that you recently took home a child that was African American."

"Uh, yes?"

"Are you fostering this child?"

"We are."

Suddenly, I felt like I was being indicted.

"And are you a white family?" She lingered on the *white* a moment too long.

I can't explain why this question rubbed me the wrong way. Why did it matter? Who gave this woman the right to bombard me with questions that seemed so judgmental? "Yes, we are," I responded, keeping my temper at bay.

"And what are your intentions for adopting this child?"

At that point, Kim and I were still telling people we hoped Cornell's biological family would come back and embrace him once he was healthy. While we bonded with him more each day, we knew our role, according to the doctors, was to "nurse him back to health and send him on his way," so to speak. I explained the plan to the person on the other end of the phone and hoped we could wrap up the interrogation. I certainly wasn't going to disclose that adoption may be a possibility. That was between Kim and me.

"Mr. Cranham." I imagined her taking off her glasses. "You are aware that by having this child in your presence, you're committing racial genocide; correct?"

"Wait, what? No, I—"

But she cut me off. "You're in the process of messing with his views of the world, and he'll likely never recover from this experience!"

I stopped trying to interrupt and sat in the nearest chair. I honestly had believed this woman was about to thank me for helping a child in need. I was trying to wrap my head around what she was saying to me, but was this actually happening? I listened as long as I could and then, something snapped within me.

"Let me tell you something." My tone shut her up. "There wasn't exactly a long line of people ready to bring this child home. He was born at twenty-three weeks, we're feeding him through a tube in his stomach, and he's breathing through another tube in his throat! Did you know that? Is that listed on whatever sheet you are looking at?" I was furious but wanted so badly to hear her response that I didn't give her the satisfaction of my hanging up.

"I was unaware of all the details, but regardless, there are far better places for this boy than with you and your wife!"

Then I did slam the phone down.

There were people and organizations that Kim and I never really felt connected to that removed us from their Christmas card list once we brought Cornell home. I had one patient who came into the office and asked to speak with me in private, either after we'd brought him home or after we adopted him. I can't recall, and it doesn't matter.

In my private office he said, "Me and my family hate what you and your wife are doing. I don't believe I can continue to give money to a doctor that would make such a choice." The hatred was filling his eyes and spilling out of his pores.

If I'm being honest, he scared me a little. I agreed that we were not the right practice for him and politely asked him to leave. I sent him right out the back door of my private office. Then I put some distance between me and this guy. What I had learned is racism and prejudice know no socioeconomic level, race, or religious boundaries. It amazed me that some of my friends and colleagues pushed us away, while total strangers welcomed our family with open arms. Some people pitied us and Cornell, others understood the wonderful gift he was for us. For Kim and me, we would not change the experience for anything. We were starting to see the world with different eyes.

It makes me recall a time when Cornell and Kaitlyn both cut their fingers at the same time on a slide at a playground we used to frequent in the mountains. Kaitlyn came running over to me crying, Cornell closely in tow. While I examined the tiny cuts, Kaitlyn abruptly stopped crying and in wonderment said, "Look, Daddy. We both bleed red!"

Truer words have never been spoken.

—∞—

Kim and I had been members of a local golf club for a few years, and at that point, I was a board member. I suppose that sounds a lot fancier than I mean it. But this was a blue-collar country club. While there were quite a few doctors and lawyers who belonged, there were also longshoremen, shipyard workers, and various types of businesspeople. From a distance, it looked like an all-encompassing place.

I met with the board on Tuesday nights. We discussed anything from events to menu options and budget issues. I liked being a part of the place and looked forward to our kids enjoying the swim team and golf lessons there, down the road.

One Tuesday afternoon, hours before our meeting, I received a phone call from the president of the board. "We gotta problem," he said. He sounded serious.

"What's going on?"

"There is a local businessman, who is coming up for membership tonight."

I knew who he was talking about. He was well known and was an extremely successful businessman in our region. As board members, we were responsible for voting in any new member. I awkwardly waited to hear more. What was the problem? I was utterly confused.

"And?" I said.

"It's a problem because this would be our first black member." I felt the nudge through the phone.

I took a minute to reflect on the club. He was right, and I'd never realized it before. The golf course did not have a single black member. It was 1996! How could that be? It did occur to me then that he would not actually be the first black member. Cornell was, now that he lived in our house. I'd never considered that if we brought him to swim in the pool, or taught him to play golf, some people would inevitably take issue with that. It seemed absurd.

"Thanks for the heads up," I told the president. "Would you mind if I said something tonight before the vote takes place? I think I can handle this one."

"Of course not. See you in a few." And we hung up.

An unusual number of members showed up to the meeting that night. Their presence made it clear the way they hoped the vote would go. The president gave me the nod to say whatever it is I wanted to say. I stood up and looked around the room. Some of these people were my friends, people I'd see on the golf course or stop to chat with before sitting down to a dinner. But now, everyone looked like Picasso versions of themselves. I was very nervous.

"I just wanted to take a moment to let you all know that the person up for discussion tonight will not be the first black member of our country club."

The crowd started looking left and then right in confusion. *What is he talking about? No one here is black!*

I pulled a picture out of my breast pocket. It was my favorite one of Cornell. "This is my son, Cornell. My wife and I brought him home recently and are very proud parents. He is part of our family. He will be going to the pool this summer, and I hope to teach him how to play golf here." I waved the photo. "This is our very first African American member." That was it. Short and sweet.

Everyone froze in their seats. It was so quiet we heard the click of the air conditioning turning on. With that, the president instructed us to vote.

The second black member was inducted into the club that night. Cornell, unbeknownst to the membership, had been the first. He would never get to enjoy that club, as I made plans to resign immediately. While I was fine with the coming repercussions, I didn't want any of the blowback directed at him.

I did some research and came across a place called Cedar Point Golf Club close by. I set up a meeting with the president before joining. I explained the makeup of my family in great detail and honesty.

"If you don't feel we will fit in well, please be frank. My wife and I have no interest in causing a stink. We just want to be welcomed. If you think we will be an issue, I will quietly go away. Please, just be honest."

The president didn't shift or clear his throat or hesitate to look me in the eye. He simply said, "We've been working, as a club, to attract and invite quality families regardless of race. We would love to have your family here."

Cornell and I enjoyed being members of Cedar Point for many, many years. While I am sure there may be a few outliers who might have had issues with our family, Cedar Point felt like home for Cornell and me. We spent some great father-son time on the links over the years at this wonderful place.

At this exact moment in time, as I am finishing this chapter, we are four days removed from the killing of George Floyd, a black man, by a white Minneapolis police officer. Our largest cities are erupting in dissent, and I am astonished that this keeps happening over and over and over again. I certainly don't have the answers. But after raising three children, two white and one black, one thing I know for sure. We are not all that different. We all need opportunity. We all need to feel valued. And we all need to give and receive love. Somehow, we have to fix the inequality.

JOHN C. CRANHAM, DDS

There is no question that our family is more accepted today than we were in 1994. Biracial couples and families are much more common. However, racism still rages on, and a large percentage of our country feels disenfranchised. I know we can live together. I *love* how my children see the world. Almost color blind. I thought I would end the chapter with an Instagram post from earlier today, by my youngest daughter, Kristen. It included a picture of all five members of our family on a beach, posing in a group hug. Then the following:

The first time I remember becoming aware of racial differences is when a little boy asked me and my sister, while at the pool, why our brother was black. I was probably in first grade and my sister responded, "why does it matter, he is our brother".

Truthfully, that was the first time I even realized he did have a different color skin than us, which speaks truth to the fact that hate is taught (but so is love). My heart hurts. Everything that is going on in our world still has yet to sink in completely, but I have been thinking about it non-stop.

Growing up in a biracial family, we have learned to combat unkind words with compassion, but I recognize that I still have so much to learn. While I will always advocate for my brother or anyone who shares his skin color, it does not mean I will ever begin to understand the struggles that they face on a daily basis. We can do so much more than we are doing. Speak up and choose love. Educate yourselves and take the time to listen to those who are hurting, they simply need to be heard. We need each other now more than ever. I see you, I hear you, I am praying for you, and I am with you.

If I have learned anything from my kids, it's to do all I can to live inclusively. It's just a better, happier, and healthier way to live. Let's hope, at some point, that our great country, particularly our leaders in both parties, will figure this out.

13

KAITLYN'S GUILT

One night when Kaitlyn and Cornell were in high school, Kim and I were lying in bed reading. She sighed and turned to me. "Does Kaitlyn seem, 'off' to you?"

I put my book down and looked at her. "She doesn't seem like herself. I agree." We were waiting for the shoe to drop with our son, but now realized that Kaitlyn was the one needing something.

"I tried to ask her what was going on, and of course, she responded, *Nothing; I'm fine*, in an exasperated tone."

"That's the memo to let you know she's a teenager now." I was making light of it, but of course, I worried about our daughter. "What's with that new friend of hers? Rachel?"

"She's trouble and a half."

"I've never known her to hang around girls like that."

Kim and I couldn't exactly pinpoint what it was about Rachel that had us on edge, but we shared the sixth sense that this wasn't going to be a healthy friendship. The girl was fourteen, going on thirty.

"Let's just keep letting her know we are here if she needs us."

As Cornell flourished during his early high school years, our concerns for Kaitlyn grew. That dark period of wanting to be left alone and hanging with a less-than-desirable crowd lasted the majority of freshman year. Kim and I respected her space. We didn't push her to talk but reminded her we were there. It was incredibly challenging to be in that role. We were concerned and wanted to help, but the only person who could do that was Kaitlyn herself.

In one way or another, Kaitlyn had kicked Rachel to the curb and started hanging out with a great group of kids. She seemed to be doing much better, but we could tell things were still eating at her. We could not, however, put our finger on them. In a conversation with Kim that summer, Kaitlyn shared some of her thoughts from the past year.

"Is it okay to be angry with God?" she asked.

"It's a relationship, and sometimes there is anger in a relationship," Kim said. "Why the anger?" Kim had to tread lightly.

"How could a loving God do what he did to Cornell and Addyson? How does he let that happen? It makes no sense."

"I think I understand; but can you be more specific?"

"Cornell can't play sports, or be in the orchestra, or get straight A's. But I can. I can do all those things, and why? Because God allows me and doesn't allow him. And what about his mother? How could she leave him at the hospital? I can't stop thinking about that—it makes me crazy! And Addy. She's a baby! Couldn't God fix her if he wanted to?"

Such good questions. We were so impressed with her critical thinking and quizzical nature.

Kim calmly explained that there are things she doesn't understand about God's ways either. And she agreed with Kaitlyn that, no, it certainly wasn't fair that she'd been given so many gifts that her brother had not. "But, with all that, I choose to continue my faith in God. I believe he loves us, even if we don't often understand him. And sometimes the difficulties we endure, may be the greatest gifts of all.

"As far as being angry with Cornell's biological mother, we don't know all the things that factored into her decision. We think we know, but we don't. Maybe you should talk to Cornell about it. I think he may be able to help you come to terms with it."

I asked Kaitlyn to give us a synopsis of what she was feeling during this time, and a glimpse of her conversation with Cornell. Her memories encompass the time frame we are speaking of, as well as the remaining years of high school. She writes:

"Growing up, Cornell was always my "twin". We were virtually the same height a lot of our childhood and learned to do a lot of things around the same time. We pushed each other. I walked first and soon after so did he. He rode a bike first and soon after so did I.

My parents always knew that I would eventually grow taller than Cornell, and also pass by him academically. It happened, in my mind rather quickly, but it could have been for so long I just really didn't notice. It was hard for me. I was always aware of Cornell's delays, but I had always seen him through child-like eyes, which meant I thought he could do everything and anything that I could.

The differences were probably clear in middle school, but they felt the most stark to me when we were in high school. I was now at least a half a foot taller than Cornell. I was in tons of clubs, was president of my class my junior year, president of my school senior year, I played sports, had dates to all of the dances, and of course started driving the second that I could. Cornell was at a different high school, so it wasn't like it was right in his face, but how could he not notice? It was such an exciting time of my life. I was hardly ever home on the weekends because of my activities or being out with friends.

The contrast with Cornell's life at that time, when I finally allowed myself to see it, was drastic. Everyone loved Cornell in school, he managed the football team and a lot of people knew who he was, but in high school people often find it hard to really find a way to connect with people who aren't the same as you. He couldn't drive and rarely got to go out. He spent a lot of time playing his music, doing his work with the teams, or just at home with my parents.

I began to feel immense guilt, all the time. I felt by living my life, and growing up, I was somehow betraying him. I knew the decisions his biological mom made and that had robbed him of what would have been a normal life in my eyes, and for that I was angry. Some of these feelings tempted me into a negative direction my Freshman year, but I managed to get past that. I was progressing and smiling, but the guilt was not going away.

These feelings reached a peak after a trip to Virginia Tech. It was a homecoming game—my first football game in Lane Stadium our senior year of High School. "Enter Sandman" was blasting over the speakers and 66,000 people were jumping up and down. I was ecstatic—I finally knew where I was going to be the following year. In the midst of all of this I looked over at Cornell wanting to share my excitement with him, and he was just kind of staring there looking around in awe. My heart shattered, because in that second, when our eyes met, we both realized and accepted simultaneously that he would never get the opportunity to experience this as a student. It felt wrong, he deserved it more than me, more than anyone. I was constantly asking "why". Why he was the one with the delays instead of me, why his mom did what she did, why the world was so unfair.

Soon after that, he was sitting at the kitchen table working on a math problem when I got home from school late one night. I looked at the problem and could solve it in my head... and he was struggling. I sat down and we had a probably two- minute conversation that changed my life forever."

"Buddy, can I talk to you for a minute?"

"Sure."

"Are you upset that I am getting to go to Virginia Tech and you aren't?"

He looked at me for a couple of seconds and finally said. "No, that's your dream school, you love Virginia Tech...I think it's awesome."

"Are you mad at your Mom? That she left you at the hospital, and did some things when she was pregnant and that's why you have a harder time learning than me?"

"No" and he paused, "We don't know what she was going through that caused her to do that. I am sure she was going through a lot."

"But your life could have been so much easier if she hadn't."

"My life is pretty great already." And he just smiled.

No anger. No resentment. Not at me, not at his mom, not at the world. I carried that for both of us for so long, and in that conversation, I realized, that was the exact opposite of what Cornell stood for, and what he wanted for me. Cornell wakes up every single day and decides to take what comes and make the absolute most of it, which would be impossible to do with a heavy heart of resentment. That doesn't mean it doesn't hurt him. It doesn't mean at times maybe he didn't wish that he could have lived differently. It means that he decided that instead of dwelling on what he can't do, he wakes up every day and decides he is going to do the absolute most with everything he has. I realized in that moment it was time to forgive. Forgive his Mom, forgive myself for growing past him, and forgive God for all that was put in Cornell's path. For the first time in a long time, I felt free.

Thankfully, Kaitlyn's bitterness had waned, and like the rest of us, she became inspired by Cornell's greatest gift: the ability to accept almost anything, and to have the full trust that it was for the best. His job was to accept things as they are, and dare I say, even be thankful for it. No matter the obstacle, it was a pattern we would see over and over again. Make no mistake, this was not taught to him. He was raised by parents whose first instinct, when something bad happens, is to wallow for a while. This was God-given—there is no other reasonable explanation. It is simply one of his greatest gifts.

14

BULLET MANAGEMENT

My son's example has helped me accept both the unexpected and the inevitable. In the early fall of 2006, I was on my way to the airport, planning to speak in Denver, when I received a phone call to head back to Richmond. My stepdad, H.D., was eighty-nine and was at the end of a tumultuous battle with obstructive coronary disease.

Over his lifetime, H.D. had endured two bypass surgeries, the replacement of his descending aorta, and the cleaning out of his coronary arteries. After his second bypass surgery in 1979, the doctors gave him five years to live. Instead of feeling like the end was near and there was no stopping it, H.D. became a model patient. He did everything the doctors told him, was an avid reader about proper nutrition, and made time for exercise. H.D. managed to live his life to the fullest and without regrets. The five years the doctors gave him turned into seventeen.

Back in April of 2006, the device that was dripping medication into his heart, a dobutamine pump, no longer functioned. We knew we didn't have a lot of time left, and the doctors advised him to get his affairs in order. All of us figured he'd make it to the fall, and that would probably be it.

H.D. followed the advice of his doctors, just as he'd done for years. He planned his own death, for lack of a better explanation, and brought his family together. Hospice was notified, and by September, H.D. was failing.

As I turned my car from the direction of the airport to that of my home, I reflected on his journey and how thankful I was to have been a part of it. My life was once on track to go in a certain direction, and it was H.D. who showed me the fork in the road and encouraged me to choose the path to greater things. Not only that, but he was a role model in every move he made throughout my life. The parallels with Cornell's influence on me only made this more poignant. I couldn't stop the tears as the miles passed.

That phone call had come on Thursday afternoon, and I was in Richmond by Friday morning. Kim, my kids, and my stepbrothers, Flip and Rob, walked together, each step crunching over the last fallen leaves that littered my parents' driveway. I held my coat together at the chest and led the pack past the familiar knocker on the front door. I couldn't help feeling nervous as I entered; certainly my emotions would be all over the board, and such vulnerability was rarely something a person like me embraced fully. I made an effort to see my stepdad often, but what would he look like, now that we were told to "hurry up and get here"?

One thing I knew: If I wanted to be sad, H.D. would embrace it. He wouldn't tell me to be happy, hold back the tears, or try to convince me he was fine. H.D. didn't run from reality and never wanted his family to do so, either. He did, however, look at this swift decline as part of the deal, and did not want us to feel bad for him. He'd had one hell of a ride!

I greeted my mom with a hug, and she led us to the living room. H.D. had been moved to a chair in there so we could have a little party that night. He didn't want people milling about through his bedroom like a bunch of zombies. There he sat in his PJ's, frail as I had ever seen him, breathing with the help of the oxygen streaming through his nasal cannula. He was a shadow of the man I once knew, but the one thing that remained was the twinkle in his eye. He was determined to put on a good show and make this festive.

Some extended family arrived that Friday night in time for dinner. We ordered in from Bonefish Grill, and I'm certain all of us were remembering the times we'd been there with H.D. in the past. Going out to dinner with him was an event, because H.D. liked to make friends with everyone—the hostess, server, bartender, the people at the next table. He believed eating was a celebration and wanted everyone to be a part of his party. His booming voice would carry over the restaurant, and I was always convinced that by the end of the meal, everyone near us secretly wished they were at our table.

That night, H.D. ate tilapia and sipped a martini, a standard combination. Now and again, he'd drift in and out of sleep, but he was mostly alert and interactive. He couldn't have weighed more than 130 pounds. He was so frail, but he was enthusiastic about all of us being together in his home. At one point, he took time to look each of us in the eye and tell us how we were special in our own way.

It got late, and all of us, particularly H.D., were tired. We said our goodnights, and my brother picked up H.D. like he was a child and put him to bed. A few hours later, H.D. died in his sleep. I'm certain if people could choose a way to go, it would be something along the lines of H.D.'s last hours.

The entire service was a result of his own planning. The parking lot we pulled into that Saturday morning was full, which was incredible in and of itself. After all, H.D. and my mom had only lived in Richmond for five years.

H.D.'s children and a few other relatives spoke on his behalf. While speaking was a part of my job, this one had me tangled up. It was one thing to discuss the ins and outs of dental occlusion, but quite another to encapsulate my stepdad's life and what it meant to me. I wasn't sure it was possible. But I remembered so many "impossible" things that my son had done that I had to try. I wanted to take everyone in the pews and put them into my skin, so they could walk around a bit with my memories and feel what he meant to me.

H.D.'s favorite poetry and scripture were read, and we sang a few songs. What I remember most about that day was exiting the church to the rousing sound of the Michigan fight song, a perfect finishing touch. H.D. had planned it to a T, and I'm certain every person exited the church feeling both exhilarated and heartbroken.

—m—

Three weeks later, with little warning, my biological father, Colin, passed away. Similar to what had happened with my sister Wendy, I had to piece together what had happened because no one wanted to talk about it. I heard there was cancer and a problem with his liver. I also learned that even the slightest physical exertion had been a struggle. He hated seeing doctors and often ignored what they had to tell him.

Our extended family headed to Arnprior, Ontario, for his funeral. As we traveled, I shared some memories of my dad with Kim and the kids. Like H.D., Dad had been a hell of an athlete. He played football at the University of Toronto as a running back, on a scholarship, and had a stint as a college football coach prior to entering his career in business. He even played on a world championships softball team in the 1940s, sponsored by the Tip Top Tailors. My biological dad had been a man's man, in many ways.

When we arrived, Dad's wife informed us of when the party at their house would take place, and that was that. There would be no church service or formal goodbye. My father had stopped believing in God years before, and therefore, he had no relationship with the Church and no desire to have a service in one. Instead, my family attended a cocktail party of about forty people who gathered together as a way to pay respects to their friend.

After our initial hellos, the kids went off to another room with other kids, Kim caught up with my brother and sister, and I slowly made my way through the house. Entering the first empty room was like a massive exhale. The floor creaked, and there was a draft coming through the window next to the ticking clock.

Was I looking for something? I don't know.

I pushed past the outdated furnishings until I made it to the back porch that overlooked the water. I had sat here with my dad many times; it was one of his most favorite spots in the world. I raised my drink, took a sip, and said in the quietest voice possible, "Cheers, Dad." I set my glass on the coffee table and said, "Goodbye, Arnprior."

The contrast of how my two fathers left the world was striking and illustrative. These events were profoundly sad, but nonetheless enlightening. H.D. had lived life in stark contrast to my father: he was a fighter, stayed positive, and chose a spiritual path that was devoid of anything that might mask his pain. I also thought of my son, and the traits he shared with H.D. He refused to give up, chose to focus on what he could do rather than what he couldn't, and held no ill will toward the people in his past who'd let him down.

At the end of 2006, I was clear about the kind of man I wanted to be, and how I wanted to be remembered when it was my time to leave the world. I learned quite a bit from my biological father, but sadly, much of it was the way I *didn't* want to be. It was my stepfather and adopted son, positioned precariously at the bookends of my life, with whom I have no blood relation, who taught and influenced me the most.

The story of my two dads reminds me of a moment that I am often drawn back too. It was 2003, and the Cranhams and the Davidsons— H.D.'s family—were having a family reunion at Smith Mountain Lake. This is a very special place for us, as Flip (H.D's oldest son) and I bought a Lakehouse there together that week, a place to which we still return today.

One day during that stay, Flip, I, and several other men went off to play a round of golf. Cornell was riding shotgun in the car in front of us. During the forty-minute car ride, Flip asked me what I thought was most remarkable about Cornell. At this time, my son was 9 years old.

I told those in the car that I marveled at his ability to dodge bullets. It seemed that they just kept coming at him from every direction, but he bobbed and weaved, without giving up. He just stayed positive and moved on. I further ventured on how different the world would be if everyone had his ability at "bullet management."

The car was quiet for a minute, and then Flip remarked, "What is different with Cornell is he has actually taken a few bullets, and he keeps moving *forward!*"

Everyone in the car laughed. Flip meant this in a positive way, as his point was that the hand Cornell had been dealt was far worse than most of ours. A few of the bullets had hit him, causing many of his deficits. It was not slowing him down… much.

But Flip missed the point entirely. While Cornell's deficits are more apparent, we *all* have bullets coming at us, and some do hit us. They come at different times. Some are emotional bullets, from our peers or family, some come from society. Some come in the form of a disease we have to fight. Some are self-inflicted. We all have scars and things we have to overcome. The most successful people just manage them better. I think of H.D., and how he'd had two wives and a girlfriend die of cancer, and then had to fight his own battles with coronary disease. Yet he was one of the happiest, emotionally intact people I have ever met.

As I left the fall of 2006 behind me, one thing was clear. H.D. had managed bullets better than my own dad. He faced things head on. I learned later that it hadn't always been like that—H.D. had grown spiritually and emotionally as he went through these events. I clearly knew H.D. at his best. The H.D. that I knew would rapidly go through the various stages of grief until he reached total acceptance of the reality of what was going on, and then he would make the best of it. The same, exact behavior seemed to be hardwired into my son. I was determined to do my best to live my life the same way.

15

TEACHING US TO LIVE GRATEFUL

The stars aligned in such a way that Kaitlyn and Cornell had their junior proms on the same night. Hard to believe, I know, but true. Keep in mind that they went to different schools in different parts of town, which made it all the more fantastic. Kaitlyn and her ever-expanding group of friends all planned a gathering for pictures beforehand.

Prom is a funny thing for parents. Before my eyes, late that Saturday afternoon, were two of my children, dressed to the nines, and looking more like real adults than little people who needed me. Cornell sported a fantastic tux that was cut to make him look as sharp as possible. Kaitlyn spent months finding the perfect dress, and she now looked as beautiful as ever.

Kaitlyn's school was in Newport News, on the other side of the Tidewater area. We asked Cornell if he'd mind getting dressed early, so we could all attend Kaitlyn's pictures together. We drove over and met by the water with about twenty couples—forty of Kaitlyn's closest friends.

The pictures went on and on. And on.

Kaitlyn with her date.

Kaitlyn with her girlfriends.

Kaitlyn with each girlfriend.

Cornell, will you take a picture of your mom, Kristen, and me with Kaitlyn?

The whole group.

Now, make a silly face.

Another picture of Kaitlyn and her date.

Cornell stood by in his tux, watching the entire time. He managed to be in a few pictures with Kaitlyn, but make no mistake about it, he was on the sidelines. Eventually, it was time for Kaitlyn's group to leave, so we kissed her goodbye, and off she went, like a princess in a Disney movie.

Cornell didn't have a prom date or a group with which to take pictures before the dance. If he was upset about that, he didn't let on. He was hungry, and said he was fine with grabbing something at a drive-through on our way back across the water. The plan was for us to drop him off at the prom, where he was to meet up with some of his buddies. Then Kim and I were going to have dinner with the parents of some of Kaitlyn's friends. It worked for us.

Once we got his belly full of his favorite Chick-Fil-A, we pulled up to the hotel in downtown Portsmouth where the dance was being held. I actually wondered if they had planned the prom in conjunction with another fancy party. Between the lights, limos, decor, and attire, it was like we'd arrived at a Hollywood red-carpet event. Hordes of stunning young people walked into the building arm in arm or glued together in small groups. There were camera flashes and laughter, lipstick touch-ups and fist-bumping.

I thought of walking that red carpet all by myself, and it intimidated me, a grown up! How was my son—so small in comparison to the others—going to do this? My heart leapt into my throat. I was terrified for Cornell.

Before I finished that thought, Cornell put his hand on the door handle, smiled at us, and said, "Here I go! I'll be right here at midnight!" He left as quickly as Kaitlyn had.

We heard the car door slam, and Cornell bounced on his toes, all the way down the carpet. He passed couples and groups but did not pick up his pace. He threw out a few waves to people along the way and disappeared through the front doors.

Kim burst into tears. I didn't need to ask what was wrong. Not only did I know, but it was too much to articulate. I watched my wife's shoulders shake, the tears stream down her face, and I joined her.

The gap between the lives of our two oldest children was so discernible that night, it was overwhelming. To be clear, neither of us was crying because we felt sorry for Cornell; quite the opposite. We were emotional at his incredible bravery. Nothing was going to stand in the way of his having a full junior prom experience. Cornell wasn't deterred by the cool kids or by whatever Kaitlyn was doing. He had no sense of entitlement that he was owed a certain experience. He had no story in is his head about how it should be. He had no interest in comparing his night to his sister's. Instead, his desire was to create a unique experience that was all his own. An experience he was *grateful* for. In order to achieve that, Cornell had to put himself out there. And he was fearless.

What did Kim and I do that night? We went and had dinner with our friends as we had planned, and we both hoped and prayed our kids were having a great time. And, of course, we worried. We were incredibly eager to hear how the night went for both kids. Kaitlyn had plans through the weekend, but midnight hit, and I pulled up to grab Cornell outside the hotel.

I didn't have to look long before my son was running toward the car with that trademark indefatigable look on his face. All I could see was teeth. He opened the door, plopped into the front seat, and said, "That. Was. Awesome!" He did not stop talking the entire trip home.

They played all my favorite songs!
The food was like, the best food I've ever had!
I danced a lot!
Mr. Paul was there!
I saw a bunch of the guys from the football and basketball team!

And on he went. It took everything in me not to start crying once again. A little later in life, I heard from others about things that Cornell didn't tell me because they hadn't occurred to him as important to share. Apparently, a couple of the "cool" girls had asked him to dance during the night. He spent time "making the rounds" to students, teachers, and all the hosts, dispensing firm handshakes, eye contact, and charisma—classic Cornell, casting his spell.

An after-party took place at the bowling alley near our house when prom was over. Cornell raced inside to his bedroom, changed his clothes, and I dropped him off again. He was there from twelve-thirty to five A.M. When I pulled into the parking lot, only a couple of cars remained. Cornell closed out the after-party. I was exhausted, but wide awake with the reassurance that Cornell had achieved the full prom experience, just as he'd wanted. From a dad's perspective, it seemed like one of the best nights in high school.

By the end of junior year, two things were clear: Kaitlyn would have her pick of whatever college or university she would like to attend, and Cornell would have no chance of going to college. I suppose that comes off more harshly than I intend, but academically, Cornell wasn't capable. The kids were on two completely different tracks. Kim and I were overjoyed for Kaitlyn. All her efforts were going to pay off, and she should bask in all of it. Our concerns for Cornell's situation were growing, however. Where would he go? What would he do after high school? We weren't exactly certain, and I'm not sure he was, either.

The next few months were, by necessity, tunnel-visioned around Kaitlyn. Kaitlyn prepped for the SATs while Cornell sat by and watched. Kaitlyn visited colleges, and Cornell sat by and watched, quietly. There were hours upon hours of conversations about which college might be the right fit for her. Often this happened around the dinner table, while Cornell sat by and listened.

Kaitlyn decided to investigate University of Virginia, James Madison, and Virginia Tech. We would go with her as a family and watch her eyes get bigger with each step. After the initial visits, she immediately ruled out UVA and was down to JMU and VT. They just fit better. Her second visit to Virginia Tech was during a football weekend, and I just so happened to stumble upon some great tickets to the game. The Hokies played Boston College. It turned out, our seats weren't far from the student section, and it was wild. We were not prepared for the immensity of it all.

The majority of people in the stadium started chanting something about ten minutes before game time. We couldn't really make it out. I'm sure our family looked around like we were seeing snow fall for the first time—wide eyes, mouths ajar, unsure of what to say or do. Then, at closer inspection, we saw the signs at center field, prompting the chants. *"Let's go!"* one side of the field chanted, as the other side chanted, *"Hokies!"* It was fan unity at its best.

Then, suddenly, the first few bars of Metallica's "Enter Sandman" started blaring over the powerful sound system, and the crowd went nuts. Sixty-five thousand fans jumped up and down in perfect unison. The earth was literally shaking as the players sprinted onto the field, right below us. Lane Stadium was erupting.

In this moment of complete insanity, with Kaitlyn jumping out of her own skin, she turned to me and yelled, "I am soooooo going here next year!" Thrilled, she'd found her place.

In that instant of pure joy, I glanced over at Cornell and caught a split-second of sadness on his face. This future was for Kaitlyn, not for him. It took him a minute, but soon enough Cornell was smiling and jumping around like the rest of us. I'd seen Cornell do this, many times before. He faced any harsh reality head on, completely accepted it, and moved on. No wallowing.

By Christmas, Kaitlyn, through the early-admission process, was accepted at VT before most of her friends had even completed an application. Our home became a whirlwind of guests and visitors with cards, gifts, VT gear, and the like. I was pumped for my oldest daughter. Kaitlyn had worked her tail off to arrive at this point, and she should be celebrated. Yet, in all the excitement, I couldn't help but worry about my son.

Cornell never showed anything but pure support and love for Kaitlyn, but I believed something more was going on, deep down. It was January—too cold for golf—when the girls were out doing something, and Cornell and I were home alone. Instead of taking him to the tees for a chat, like usual, I asked him to sit down with me in the family room.

"Cornell, how're you doing?" I tried to sound casual, but we both saw right through it. I felt off.

He looked at me and kind of raised one eyebrow. "Fine."

I needed to be more specific. "Cornell, a lot of very exciting things are going on with Kaitlyn, and I know that you understand that college is not in your future." I cleared my throat and leaned forward a bit.

My son stared at me.

I waited, but no response. So, I tried again. "You know Kaitlyn is going to Virginia Tech. How do you feel about that?"

When he spoke, I felt like we'd made it over some type of intangible barrier. "I'm excited for Kaitlyn. She loves it there, and we'll be able to go visit her and see football games. I think she'll do really well. It's going to be awesome."

Not what I was looking for, so I continued, "I know that Kaitlyn will do well. But…" I shifted in my chair. "Do you ever think about going to college?" I felt like this was a parenting moment I'd read about in a book, and I was miserably trying to do what the authors suggested.

Cornell looked at me like I'd just suggested he run away and join the circus. "Dad, I'm not going to college."

I decided to throw the hypothetical book out the window. "Cornell, I know you're not going to college. But, with everything going on with Kaitlyn, I just want to know how you're doing. I want you to know it's okay to feel sad that you aren't going to college. And, if you need to, we can talk about it."

There, that's what I had been trying to say.

Cornell held my gaze and looked at me with the most serious expression I'd ever seen. Fifteen or twenty silent seconds hung in the air, as if he were purposely doing it for the eventual effect. Then he said, "Dad: *would that help?*"

Touché. I sat in silence for a minute, reflecting on such a question. Finally, I managed to respond, "Well, actually, no."

He went on, "Dad, I'm happy. Kaitlyn has things that she can do that I can't, and I have things that I can do that she can't. Virginia Tech is the right place for her, and I'll find the right place for me. You don't need to worry about me. I'm good."

Translation: *Dad, don't waste my time stating the obvious. I moved on from this years ago. I have my own path and am grateful to see what God has in store for me. Get out of my face.*

And that was that.

When we brought Cornell home all those years ago, it would have been impossible to add him to our insurance. Understandably, no company in its right mind would have taken the risk. In the off chance that someone did accept us, the premiums would have been so high due to his preexisting condition that the bills would have been unaffordable.

The Department of Social Services stepped in and ended up playing a pivotal role in helping us make sense out of our options. We sat down with a few people who recommended something called an "assisted adoption," which allowed us to retain his Medicaid status for his health insurance, yet still adopt him. I'm not sure we could have pulled it off, otherwise. Throughout the years, the department was also instrumental in helping us receive various other services for Cornell.

Several months after Cornell completed high school, one of his social workers wanted to have a meeting with us. By this time, Cornell was working at Bay View Dental Lab, learning the skills of mounting models for teeth restorations and helping our good friend Angelo, who works there. Cornell was loving it. So, after work, Cornell and I were off to meet with his social worker, who had been following his care. I anticipated this to be nothing more than a progress report.

"Cornell, I wanted to call a meeting to make sure you understand all of your options, now that you've graduated high school."

We waited.

"We want to make it clear that you will continue to have any number of resources available to you, given your diagnosis. You know, should you be unable to find work."

Cornell was about to interrupt to say he had a job, but I wanted his social worker to finish his thought first. "Hang on," I whispered.

The social worker continued, "You're entitled to a monthly check." He then shifted his gaze back and forth to Cornell and me. "And it's enough money for you to live on your own."

"I appreciate you taking the time to let us know all our options," I said. "But Cornell has a job, at Bay View Dental Lab." I smiled proudly.

The social worker raised his eyebrows. "That's really great, Cornell. But keep in mind, this is a substantial amount of money each month, simply given to you, if you cannot find work."

I said, "To be clear, people in dental labs make pretty good money. Many of the support people can go on to assist the ceramists in a dental lab, or get a job in a dental office. We are hoping that, at some point, he can come and help me in my dental office, and eventually work with his sister, who is planning on going to dental school."

The social worker sat there, trying to take this all in, seemingly getting frustrated by our resistance. Cornell was still trying to grasp what was going on.

"I have a question," Cornell said. "So, am I going to work for the government? Where would I go to work?"

Apparently, he couldn't wrap his head around the fact that the government would simply cut him a check because he had been sick as a little boy.

"No, you don't understand," the supervisor spoke up. "You wouldn't have to do anything to receive the money, except quit your job."

Cornell was still trying to logically piece this puzzle together. In his mind, he'd overcome the odds. He'd beaten it. His issues were in the past—a distant memory. I could feel the anxiety welling up inside of me. After pausing for a second, he stammered, "Where would I go? What would I do all day? I love working."

The social worker, on autopilot now, made a few more attempts to push the agenda. Of course, the intentions were good; he was trying to do the things he had been trained to do. I don't think he was prepared for the conversation to take the turn it had, but just as it made no sense to him for someone to turn down a handout, it made no sense for Cornell to take one.

At that point, I intervened. "Cornell, would you mind washing your hands for a minute? I need to speak to our friend in private."

"Sure." And off he went.

I laid into the man. "Are you kidding me right now? We have worked his whole life, *together,* to get Cornell to a point where he can be independent. We are almost there! You want him to stay home and not work? Not develop, kill his spirit?" My need to defend my son took over. "Do you know he is the first one up in our house every, single day? Five-thirty every morning, I wake up to the sound of him making his lunch. He cannot wait to go to work. What good could possibly come of him sitting around the house with nothing to do? I know we have things he still needs to learn... driving is still an issue, but let's not squash it right now!"

"Mr. Cranham, it is my responsibility to let Cornell know what he is entitled to, and I know it makes you uncomfortable but..."

Just then, Cornell walked back to the table. His hands were immaculate.

We knew the meeting was over when Cornell turned his attention back to the man in front of us, and my son's demeanor had completely changed. The consternation was gone, and the twinkle was back in his eye. He smiled and calmly said, *"Maybe you can give that money to someone who needs it."*

It was, hands down, one of the proudest parenting moments in my life. I sat back and beamed.

—⁂—

I am not suggesting that it is wrong for someone to take a subsidy from the government, a church, or a charity. We have a safety net in this country for a reason. Early on, the safety net saved Cornell's life. It is entirely possible that, someday, he may need some additional assistance. But there is a difference between receiving an entitlement and feeling entitled.

Cornell, more than anything, wants to be a contributor. He wants to be a part of something and be good at things. It gives him his self-esteem and demonstrates his value to others. People who feel entitled and are simply given things, don't have that. People who are entitled don't feel gratitude. As I move forward, with my son, we will always work toward creating the opportunities for him to be a contributor, and for opportunities for him to be grateful. It's a primary goal that Kim and I want for all our kids.

16

THE DRIVE TO DRIVE

When my stepfather sat me down and gave me the talk of all talks, I was eighteen years old and just finishing high school. As a student, I had struggled. I don't know if it was my parents' divorce, my dad moving away, or what it was, but I was living with some turmoil. There was a dark side to how I was feeling that I couldn't seem to escape. In hindsight, I suppose I was dealing with mild to moderate depression.

"John," H.D. said, "you and I both know you have yet to really apply yourself."

He was looking me square in the eye.

"What you have now is a clean slate. As you go off to college, none of the past matters. I know things have been pretty tough on you, but if you go to college and really apply yourself, I know you can create whatever future you desire. Give it one semester. Give it all you got. Let's see what happens. I bet you surprise yourself."

I sat there in silence. He could tell I needed something more.

"Let me tell you about the 3 P's. Your first job is to lock into a Purpose. Set a goal. What would you love to do the rest of your life?" I didn't answer. "Take some time to think about that, but don't undersell yourself here, think big."

This was a new concept for me, something no one had ever approached me with.

He went on. "The second P is Passion. The way you will know you have the right Purpose, or goal, is you will feel Passion for it." His eyes danced. "It will eject you out of bed in the morning! It will make you want to move around obstacles in the way."

He paused and made me wait for the last one. Then he said, "And the third P, which is most important, is Persistence. We live in a fast-food world, where everyone wants life to come fast and easy. It doesn't work like that. Things are going to get tough. You will have great challenges to overcome." Somehow, he made this sound like a pro, not a con. "Remember, this is a marathon, not a sprint. The person who can stick it out the longest often gets the prize."

I don't know why I chose to absorb those words at eighteen, but they inspired me with the possibility of what could be. To this day, I remember every word he said—and that was fifty years ago! I had never cracked a 3.0 in high school, but that year in college, I came home with a 4.0 the first semester. Still, while the words had a profound impact on me, I didn't really understand them fully. That is, until the Cornell Effect was in full swing.

—✦—

Before his last year of high school ended, Cornell's social worker mentioned a place called Woodrow Wilson Rehabilitation Center in Fisherville, Virginia. Cornell came home and told us about the facility, which helped people with physical and mental disabilities mainstream into society. "My social worker said I should look into it," he said and shrugged.

Kim and I took to the Internet. Woodrow Wilson Rehabilitation Center was a hospital that had been built after World War II. Sixty-some years later, it served as a bridge for people like Cornell, and we jumped on it. Cornell was on board, too, as long as he didn't have to quit his responsibilities at Bay View.

The initial step was a one-day assessment, which Cornell completed the week after high school graduation. It's funny how I've raced right by graduation in telling his story. It was what you'd expect for our two "twins"—parties, grand ceremonies, gift cards, and the like. I suppose there was so much excitement on the horizon that we all focused on what was ahead rather quickly.

Soon after the assessment, Cornell was invited back for a six-week life skills program at Woodrow Wilson. He was expected to start at the end of the summer, and from a father's perspective, the timing could not have been better. Two weeks after we dropped off Kaitlyn at college, we dropped off Cornell at Woodrow Wilson.

Ensconcing Kaitlyn at Virginia Tech had been like something out of a movie. The sky that day was an iridescent blue, the grass a sea of green, and everyone we met was kind and helpful: *park here; take a left to your dorm; here's a welcome package; your roommate is the nicest person in the universe.*

While it was hard to miss Kaitlyn's excitement as we moved her in, leaving her was a moment I will never forget. Kaitlyn was alone in her dorm room with Kim, Kristen and her best friend, Kayla, Cornell, and me. We were all standing around looking at each other, when someone mentioned it was probably time to go. We thought having Kayla there would help us hold things together. But, all of a sudden, *she* burst into tears. We all lost it. After a bit, we said our goodbyes and were on our way. Tears streamed down Kim's cheeks for the next several hours.

"It's kinda weird we're just leaving her there," Kristen mumbled from the backseat.

"Totally," Cornell agreed.

Two weeks later, we did it all again, but it was quite a bit different with Cornell. Virginia Tech was a sprawling campus of great beauty. The "Hokie" stone—a unique limestone used to handcraft the architectural bricks on the VT campus—is stunning. Woodrow Wilson, by contrast, looked more like a colorless institution. Don't get me wrong, the surrounding grounds are well kept, and the mountains in the distance lovely. But it lacked the lushness of VT. If Cornell noticed, he didn't let on. He was thrilled to be attending his own version of college, just like his sister, and you could tell he had a feeling these six weeks would lead to something good. Once again, never comparing.

We set Cornell up in his dorm and met his roommate, a kid about Cornell's age from up North who seemed nice as could be. When he felt comfortable, we walked the grounds, discovered the dining hall, and strolled the area around the academic buildings. It wasn't flashy, and nothing made you say wow. But, to Cornell, it was his, and it was perfect.

The three of us hugged. Cornell didn't seem the least bit nervous. I couldn't say the same. I wondered if we were subconsciously doing the same dance over and over, me, the worrisome parent, and Cornell, the son I needed to never worry about.

As we drove away, I said to Kristen, alone in the backseat, "It's weird we're leaving him there, isn't it?"

"Totally," she mumbled, still gazing out the window where she'd last seen him. A quick glance at Kim revealed the same gentle stream flowing down her cheeks.

Kim and I were thrilled for our kids, but at times, it felt like our hearts were being ripped out. I suppose that's dramatic. But within two weeks, we went from three teenagers in the house to one. Kristen was torn, too. On the one hand, she was pumped to have full reign over everything. But it was awfully lonely. We all needed time to adjust.

A few days in, Cornell called. He assured us all was well, and he was having a great time. He said he'd been hanging out with his roommate mostly and was just starting to meet other kids in his hall.

It occurred to me that for the first time in Cornell's life, he was surrounded by equals. For much of his life, Cornell had been stuck in a No Man's Land—stuck between the regular population and those who truly could not function. Just about every kid at Woodrow Wilson was in that Cornell spot. For the first time, Cornell had true peers.

In Cornell's classes, he learned autonomous life skills: balancing a checkbook, depositing and withdrawing money at the bank, washing his clothes, learning to interview, and shopping at the grocery store. He took a lot of tests to see what his strengths were. He also completed basic testing to see if he possessed the skill set to drive… something he was *very* focused on.

When Cornell's six weeks were finished, he said his goodbyes, got some cell phone numbers, and said he would do his best to keep in touch with his new friends. A few of them even lived in our area. There was more good news. Cornell was approved to take the classes to obtain his driver's license! All of us were elated. The ability to drive a car, independently, would open up a whole new world for my son.

The other positive aspect of leaving Woodrow Wilson was that Cornell had a job to return to at home. He went back to days with Angelo at the lab. Sometime in the first week of being back at it, he was making his lunch early in the morning. As I entered the kitchen, he turned and looked at me. "Dad, I just want to say, thanks."

"For what?" I asked. I couldn't imagine what he was about to say.

"I was one of the only people at Woodrow who had a job to do when classes ended. I don't know if that would be the case without your help. So, thanks."

"I only set you up with an interview. You got yourself the job."

Cornell smiled, and the two of us were off to work.

In January of 2014, we dropped Cornell off at Woodrow Wilson, just like we had in the fall. He moved back into the dorms and resumed classes and eating in the dining hall. He was pumped to be returning. This time, he had a specific goal in mind: pass the driver's test.

This would be a game changer for Cornell. Being employed and being able to drive were essential if Cornell were to have a chance at independence. This was something he was acutely aware of. Getting his license became his Big, Hairy, Audacious Goal—as Jim Collins counsels in this book, *Good to Great.* I recognized his BHAG as his Purpose, one that he felt incredible Passion for. That set him up well for achieving it.

The first task on the agenda was for Cornell to obtain his learner's permit, which would require him to pass the written test. Keep in mind that through middle school and high school, Cornell took a combination of regular classes and those aimed at kids with learning disabilities. His ability to succeed with standardized testing was almost nonexistent. I was confident he had the motor coordination to drive a car, but how would he ever pass the written test? The thought of Cornell sitting in front of a computer screen and clicking a mouse to answer questions for any amount of time was a very foreign concept.

His schedule at Woodrow Wilson revolved around taking classes for three weeks to master the information and learn the necessary skills to pass the standardized permit test. On the fourth week, Cornell would be taken over to the DMV to take the written test.

At home, Kim and I frantically Googled the tests he would be taking so we'd be able to talk to him about each section when it was over. We had no idea what to expect. How hard would such a test be for him? It was tough to gauge. I suppose I was most concerned about his reaction if he didn't pass. He had no experience with receiving a low grade in something.

The fourth week rolled around, and Kim and I had that same feeling as the night we'd dropped Cornell off at prom: we were terrified. The night before, on the phone, Cornell had assured us that he felt ready, and we told him how proud we were to hear that.

When the clock hit ten the next morning, we knew Cornell was most likely starting his test. The first ten questions were traffic sign questions. He would need to score 100 percent in order to move on to the remaining questions. I hate to state the obvious, but there was no room for error, and that was an insane concept for a kid like Cornell.

When he called, I grabbed the phone on ring one. "How did it go?"

There was a pause. Kim huddled next to me so she could hear him.

Finally, Cornell spoke. "I got seven out of ten right."

Interesting. If you looked at the situation on paper, you'd know Cornell didn't come close to passing the first section. However, the fact that he didn't call and tell us he failed, or have a negative attitude about the experience, was no small victory.

"How do you feel?" Kim asked him gently.

"I'm okay. I'm going back tomorrow to take it again."

"Great idea. Keep it fresh in your mind."

On the second day, Cornell knew eight out of ten signs. An improvement, but he still couldn't move on to part two. The third day, Cornell received a 100 percent on the sign section, but missed nearly half the questions on part two. Cornell would need an 80 percent, overall, to pass.

Midweek, I sat on the couch with Kristen in front of the television, the chatter from *Say Yes to the Dress* looming somewhere in the background of my thoughts. "Tomorrow is your brother's last day at Woodrow to take the test," I said to her.

"Can he take it again, even if he leaves Woodrow? Like, can he take it while living here?" Kristen was clearly ready for Cornell to come home.

"He can, but it would be nice if he could do it while there because of all the support surrounding him." I felt like I had to do something. "I'm going to call him," I said, excusing myself from the couch fest and grabbing my phone. When Cornell answered, I said, "How is the studying going?"

"It's going. I'm looking over things one more time tonight, and then one more time in the morning before I take the test again. I am going to get up at six, go for a walk, listen to my favorite songs, and go pass this thing!" He sounded methodical, without an ounce of discouragement.

Later that night, I received a text: *dad i can tell u r worried about me but i am fine. all this extra work is just going to make it that much more special when i pass. i love u.*

Cornell's last day at Woodrow, he missed passing by one question. One! I could have ripped my hair out! Kim picked him up, and I believe the conversation went something like this:

"How did it go?"

"I got a 79."

"Honey! That's a great score!"

"Yeah."

"If you're up to it, I'll study with you so you can keep taking it until you get the score you need. How does that sound?"

"I like that plan."

I came home that Thursday night to find them studying. Cornell could only take the written test once a day, so he was preparing for the next morning. However, when the next morning arrived, with the new environment and all, Cornell had taken a few steps back, winding up with a 75 percent. None of us worried, least of all, Cornell. He and Kim were back at the kitchen table Friday night. They both looked weary, but they kept at it. They seemed to have a good rhythm going, so I left them to it.

Saturday morning, Kim and Cornell drove to the closest DMV. They went early enough that the total craziness of a Saturday at the branch hadn't set in just yet. Cornell marched up to the front counter and was led to the testing area. Kim sat in one of the stiff plastic chairs, biting her nails and fussing with her phone.

I was giving a lecture at Bay View that morning to a study club. I kept my phone on the podium but put it on silent mode. I was hoping a text would come through that I could glance at quickly for an update.

Later, Kim told me that she worried and prayed, worried and prayed. Her stomach was in all sorts of knots, when she looked up and saw Cornell walking up to the front of the DMV. He glanced at her, alone amongst the many chairs, smiled nonchalantly, and gave her a thumbs-up.

The sixth time was a charm.

With tears in her eyes, Kim sent me a text that came through mid-lecture: *HE PASSED!!!*

I happened to glance down at my phone when it lit up, and I froze. I mean, I was in the middle of a sentence. I looked up and people could tell something was up. In fact, I think most worried I'd received a text that someone had died. The only words I could find were, "Excuse me," as I stepped away from my post. It was one of those rare moments in which I was so happy but couldn't stop the tears. I grabbed a few tissues, cleaned myself up, and returned to the group.

"I apologize. If we can just break topic for a moment, so I can share some news…."

Everyone's shoulders sort of dropped as they switched positions in their chairs, not knowing where I was going with this.

"My son, Cornell, has been studying for the past month to pass the driver's test for a learner's permit." I could feel the tears coming again but stopped them in their tracks. "He's taken it six times. And now, this morning, he passed!"

After a beat, the room of 20 gave me and my son a warm round of applause. This particular group all knew of Cornell and his struggles, to some degree, and they were genuinely happy for him. It was awesome.

Cornell returned to work at Bay View but went back to Woodrow Wilson in April of 2015 to work on the road portion of his driving. He'd have a few more weeks at this favorite place of his to do nothing but focus on his driving. This was important, as he needed to get cleared by the driving professionals at Woodrow in order to be granted his license. We wanted to be 100 percent sure he would be safe on the road, for himself and others.

As always, it was a slow, laborious process. He clearly had the coordination and skill but finding out how to set up a car to fit his size was important. They soon discovered that sitting on a pillow and using pedal extenders made a big difference in helping him see properly, as well as putting him in the proper position in relation to the steering wheel. Quite simply, cars don't fit four-foot, eleven-inch people very well.

At the end of the three weeks, they were not yet ready to release his license. They wanted us to drive with him, and to see him come back in six months for another evaluation. *Six months!* Again, the decision didn't seem to faze Cornell. They were specific that he did best when he was driving in familiar areas, so they suggested we start driving with him to and from work, and anywhere else he would like to go—like, maybe, the golf course. They reassured us that he was very close to being proficient. He just needed to make sure he saw and acknowledged all the traffic signs, and developed better situational awareness around the car, particularly when merging into traffic. They also suggested he get a car of his own that he could consistently drive.

So, with that, we began the final push. First step: car shopping. Cornell had diligently saved his money and was ready. Kim and Cornell went to CarMax and came home with a bright-blue, 2011 Ford Escape. He wrote a check for ten thousand dollars and secured a loan for five thousand more, in order to have a small car payment and to start developing his own credit. We were so proud of our young man!

By this time, Cornell had left Bay View and was at a new job in Virginia Beach, twenty-one miles away. We mapped out a route, avoiding the interstates and the majority of traffic, so that Kim and I could both supervise his driving each day. Cornell would drive with Kim to his new dental lab; she would then take his car to my office, leave it there, and drive my car home. At the end of my day, I would take Cornell's car to pick him up from work, and then he would drive us both home. It added ninety minutes to our commutes, but Kim and I felt it was worth it, if Cornell could be successful.

He went back to Woodrow Wilson in January of 2016 to pursue his full license. This second time, Cornell sailed right through. They granted him his driver's license. Purpose, Passion and incredible Persistence, personified.

When he came home, Kim was not completely ready for him to do the solo thing to work. We let him drive on his own to places closer to home, gradually extending the distance. Finally, in April 2016, Cornell pulled out of the driveway for the first time to head to work by himself. I don't know who was more excited, Cornell or me, as I had just got ninety minutes of my life back each day! In all seriousness, this was a moment we had prayed for his entire life. It would be very difficult to be independent without this skill.

The 3 P's were alive and well during the push to get his license. The Purpose was clear. He wanted to drive. He knew that if he were going to have a shot at an independent life, driving would be a key component. That provided the Passion. The purpose and passion led to ridiculously Persistent behavior.

I remember hitting balls on a driving range with Cornell when he was about fifteen. We were there with a buddy of mine, Matt Angelelli, and his son, Chris. Chris was five years younger than my son, and over the years they'd developed a nice friendship. We all knew that Chris would shoot right by Cornell at some point, and even then, Chris was bigger, and his game was better. But as always, the comparison didn't seem to matter to Cornell.

Matt is a Psychiatrist and, by nature, studies human behavior. I will never forget the observation he made on that piping hot, Virginia afternoon.

"What is so amazing about your son is, he doesn't have a story in his head."

"What do you mean?" I asked.

"He is just relentless in how he goes after his own life. He has completely accepted all of the crap that has happened to him, and it doesn't seem to bother him a bit. I keep looking for evidence of resentment, bitterness, or anger, and it doesn't exist," he marveled. "Things come far easier to his siblings and friends, and he just doesn't seem to care. And it's not like he isn't cognitively able to know that, by comparison, he is behind. He doesn't feel the world owes him anything, he just works on things at his own pace and seems to be thrilled about it. It is amazing, man."

I smiled knowingly, and watched my son hit balls.

17

ARIEL

As Cornell grew, occasionally he would ask about his biological family. Dr. W, his child psychologist, had recommended that we wait until he reached twenty-one before he tried to make any connection with them, should he want to do so. At that stage, she explained, he'd be fully developed emotionally and able to handle whatever may be on the other side. You could tell she was speaking from experience.

So, when Cornell asked, I'd say, "Buddy, when you're twenty-one, if you want us to help you find your biological family, we will do so." He would nod and go about his business. We were never 100 percent sure what was going on in his head.

Then, one evening after bible study, now twenty-five years old, he dropped this bombshell.

He addressed Kim and me. "So, we took turns telling our story tonight at bible study. I told them all about you, and how I was sick when I was little, and how you adopted me. That I almost died… and I also told them about Ariel, my twin."

I would have loved to have been a fly on the wall that night. Cornell rarely looks backward.

"One of my friends came up afterwards and asked me some more questions about Ariel. He said he was pretty good with a computer, and that if I wanted, he could help me find her. Her name is Ariel Richardson, right?"

"Yes, that's right. What did you say?" Kim stammered.

"I told him I thought it might be time to meet her."

Kim and I just sat there a little bit dazed.

And then I said, "Well, we always told you we would help you once you were twenty-one. You are more than old enough now, if you want to look for her. We'll get to work on it tomorrow."

Tomorrow came, and I had a large reconstruction case to do. I was up to my elbows from seven to eleven that morning. Recently, Cornell had left his second job at the dental lab in Virginia Beach and was now working with me. He was doing some of our laboratory work in-house, and found he was good at some of the digital workflows I needed to have done prior to treatment-planning my cases. Cornell liked following detailed protocols and did not get bored with repetitive tasks.

About 10:45 A.M., I was finishing my case, and I noticed him standing outside the door of operatory #1. He looked as though he had seen a ghost. He was staring at me and pointing at his phone. I walked into the hall to see what was going on.

"Dad, look at this."

It was a text message from his buddy. It read: *Dude I think I found your sister.*

As I scrolled downward, I saw screenshots from the Facebook page of a young woman who looked eerily similar to the young man in front of me. Her name, Ariel Richardson. What put a lump in my throat is, over the years, on October second, their birthday, she would post the one picture she had of him, an extremely weathered photo from the NIQU, and a simple statement: *Cornell, I know you are out there, I love you, I miss you, and one day I will find you. Happy Birthday!*

I looked up to see tears in Cornell's eyes and a huge smile on his face.

The next twenty-four hours are a blur. I know I called Kim and the girls. Phone calls and text messages were flying back and forth among our extended family. The emotions were happiness for Cornell, but also fear that we somehow might lose him. Would he want to be with them more than us? Stupid, selfish emotions that were impossible not to feel. I did my best to push them aside.

A promise, however, was a promise, and we embraced the opportunity to connect with Ariel. I can't explain it, but I began to have a consistent, positive feeling about what was going to take place.

"What do you want to do? I asked.

I half expected him to email TMZ, Dr. Phil, Maury Povich, or Ellen. Maybe one of them could televise this great reveal! Isn't that what our culture does now? I expected him to be impulsive, to jump on Facebook and immediately reach out to his long-lost twin. But that didn't happen.

Instead, he simply waited. The first week went by, and he quietly went about his business, a little quieter than normal. The second week went by, and Kim and I were getting concerned.

"Are you *okay*, buddy? she asked. "We are concerned about you; can we help?"

"I am fine. I'm just trying to figure all this out."

Weeks turned to months, and we started to think he might never act on this. Occasionally, we would discuss the elephant in the room, but generally, he was tight-lipped about the whole thing. He was not brooding or depressed, just very focused and serious.

One day, that changed. He walked into our room before bed one evening and said, "I have been thinking about Ariel nonstop. I guess I just don't know what to do next. I don't know what it is, but I am worried about some things, and I don't really even know what they are, or why I'm worried. I am thinking maybe I could talk to somebody about it."

We weren't expecting this.

"Absolutely!" Kim said, offering our support. "This is a lot. We can definitely help you find someone. Maybe we can reach out to your pastor, or maybe we can find a family therapist that knows about things like this."

I sat back and, once again, was blown away by my son's depth. The emotional intelligence he was exuding was off the charts. Way beyond what his intellectual capacity should have allowed him to compute. But he knew he needed help, and he was not afraid to ask for it. Something we can all learn from.

In the coming months, Kim found a family therapist in Virginia Beach. It was a shock, at the first visit, to find that we were not going to be with Cornell in these therapy sessions. He was an adult, and we clearly were not invited. The therapist thought it was going to be more productive without us. It got our noses a little out of joint, but we reluctantly agreed.

Over the next several months, Cornell would make the forty-mile round trip, after work, in rush-hour traffic. All we know about those sessions was what he told us, which wasn't much. We could see they seemed to be helping. He was far less distracted, happy with the sessions, and kept telling us that he would let us know when it was time to reach out to Ariel.

Then, one day at the end of November 2018, he announced it was time. Cornell had waited almost a year to get things in order. When we asked him why he was ready, it was pretty simple.

"Me and my therapist spent a lot of time talking about what might happen. That it could be great, or it might not be. We sort of talked through all the different possible things that could happen, so I wouldn't be surprised."

I would have loved to know what those were.

"I am ready to accept the good and the bad now. I also understand that I can set the boundaries for what happens. I am not sure who in my biological family I want to meet, and that is okay. All I know is, I want to have a relationship with Ariel for now, and it's okay for me to tell her that. I just want things to go slow. So, I need help with writing her a letter, and then we are going have a talk on the phone. After that, my therapist is recommending we meet somewhere, maybe at a restaurant."

So, that was it. He did a really nice job on the letter. We did some light editing and double-checked that it was exactly what he wanted to say.

"That's it!" he said with a big grin.

He sent her a note on Facebook messenger with his cell phone number. Then we all waited on pins and needles. We expected to hear something immediately. Then, a week had gone by, and nothing. Kim and I were starting to get concerned. Had she changed her mind about wanting to meet him? How bad would this hurt him if she had?

Then, one day, he mentioned that someone kept calling him from a number he didn't know. That was so Cornell.

I'm like, *"Dude,* that is probably her!"

He stared at his phone and said, "Maybe I can send a text message to that phone and ask who it is."

"Good idea."

Within five minutes, Cornell and his twin sister were texting back and forth. They agreed to chat on the following day, when he knew he would be on the drive with me to our Lakehouse. From his perspective, it was a nice block of uninterrupted time; from my perspective, a perfect time for me to hear one side of this epic conversation!

The Call was scheduled for 2:00 in the afternoon. At 1:55, we were somewhere between Petersburg and the little town of Crewe on Route 460. As the seconds got close to crunch time, I could feel the anxiety rising in my son. He kept shifting his position in his seat.

"How are you doing, man?"

He glanced over at me, with those dimples framing the corner of his mouth. He tilted his head a little to the left and let out a huge sigh. Something I have seen a thousand times.

"Shit is about to get real."

Cornell is rarely one to cuss, so I busted out laughing.

"Dad, seriously, this seemed easier when I was talking to my therapist, but now it's all jumbled in my head, I…"

Then the phone in his hand started ringing.

Then it rang again. And again.

"Are you going to answer it? I think we know who it is," I said with a smile.

"Hello…"

Then I heard a blood-curdling scream of joy coming through the phone.

For the next hour, they talked. More like Ariel talked, and Cornell answered questions. The entire time, he was grinning from ear to ear. The coolest thing he learned that day is that he was an uncle. Jazmine, his niece, was three years old at the time, and he even got to talk to her for a while.

"Do you have a pony?" Jazmine asked. Random, I know, but it cracked Cornell up.

Due to the fact that so little of the conversation was on our end, I still don't know everything they were talking about. But I do know he was happy, and I do know it had a positive effect on him—as though it filled some long-lost void that, maybe, only twins completely understand. It was both beautiful and beyond cool.

Over the next few weeks, Cornell and Ariel would continue to talk almost daily. They learned they had been very close to one another multiple times. She had attended Cornell's rival high school, Oscar Smith. It was a regional high school powerhouse, and Western Branch's sports nemesis. Cornell loved it when they played OS. Their fans were electric, and often it was a great game. When Cornell was on the visitors' sidelines, Ariel had been in the stands on the other side of the field, less than a hundred yards away. They found out that Ariel had worked literally down the street from Bay View Dental Lab, a few blocks from Cornell's first job. It was all pretty amazing.

The first in-person meeting happened at the Red Robin near my office. Kim, me, Cornell, Ariel, and Big Jerry, her fiancé, were in attendance.

Our crew arrived first. And a few minutes later, Ariel and Jerry walked in. She was very easy to spot. She and Cornell stood there and awkwardly looked at each other for a few seconds.

Then Jerry said, "Well ya'll should hug or something!"

That broke the ice. Hugs all around.

What started as somewhat awkward soon normalized, and today it is like the twins were never apart. They talk or text almost daily and try to get together a couple of times a month. Most recently they celebrated their 28th birthday, together.

For Cornell, it has to be so wonderful, to know that he was missed. Circumstances just didn't allow for the family to take care of him, but that did not mean they did not care about him or miss him. While he never articulated feelings of abandonment or feeling hurt, they must have been a part of him. Now those feelings were gone.

I give Cornell tremendous credit for the time he took to get ready for such a soul-stirring event. It takes courage and a high degree of emotional intelligence to know when you need help. It's a principle I need to remember, as too often, I will put my head down and go it alone.

18

CORNELL'S GREATEST GIFT

In 2013, we vacationed in Destin, Florida. It was Kristen's spring break and those vast, white sandy beaches sounded like just the thing for all of us. I always love that moment when exiting the Florida airport, the way the humid air rushes up toward you. It lets me know I've arrived and am truly on vacation.

We rented a condo on the beach that had four golf courses on-site. Everyone was happy; the girls did the pool and beach all day, while Cornell and I soaked up the greens. We played golf like fiends every day. We hit eighteen each morning and practiced for an hour or two in the early afternoon. By about three o'clock, we'd all meet up and spend the rest of the day together.

On our last day, Cornell and I were headed in from our favorite of the four courses, when I looked down at my left knee. It had blown up like a balloon, and if I weren't careful how I moved, it was fairly painful. The most disheartening part of such a realization wasn't the knee itself, but the fact that I couldn't push my body the way I used to. *Since when can't I play golf every day without consequence?* I felt weak. Frustrated. Embarrassed. In my mind, I was still twenty-five. My knee told me otherwise.

I figured I'd torn a meniscus or something along those lines. When we returned to Virginia, I made sure to ice and rest it. Eventually, I was tired of hobbling around and made an appointment with an orthopedic surgeon.

After x-rays and scans, the doctor gave me the "Do you want the good news or the bad news first?" routine, as I had done with a thousand patients.

"You pick."

"Good news is, you didn't tear your meniscus. Bad news is, you have osteoarthritis."

I was, of course, aware of this condition, one that mostly afflicted *old guys.*

"The cartilage at the end of your bones has worn down, and it is not a question of 'if' you are going to need a knee replacement, it is a matter of 'when.'"

"How long can I put it off?" I didn't want to stop moving forward, in anything I did. Something like this was sure to set me back.

"If you want to postpone it as long as possible, you need to completely stop any high-impact activities."

Of all the things I do, the first two activities that entered my mind were running, and attempting to jump the wake on the wakeboard. I'd have to put a pause on all that.

I hobbled out of the office like a sad sack walking a hypothetical plank. It was all downhill from here. *I'm old, used, damaged goods,* I thought. My kids wouldn't look at me the same. I'd have to "sit this one out" more times than not. And vacations would have everyone involved whispering, "Can old Dad still do that?"

I was now officially a geezer. I allowed my pity party to continue unabated.

Early the next Saturday morning, Cornell cruised down the stairs. Normally, he says good morning first thing, but apparently not today. "What's wrong with you?" he asked, reading my sour expression.

"Me?"

"No, the other guy looking pitiful." Cornell smiled.

He pulled up a chair, and I told him about my doctor's appointment. I explained that my knee was in bad shape and would need to be replaced at some point. I had to ease up on the running, wakeboarding, and so on. I told him everything.

Cornell sat and listened. Not once did he attempt to interrupt, and when I was finished, he remained quiet. I could tell he was processing something, so I let him be. His expression wasn't altered when he finally spoke.

"What can you still do with your hurt knee?" Before I could answer he continued, "Hang on a second...." and zipped out of the room. He returned moments later with a sheet of paper in his hand and that calm, confident smile I love so much. And I knew I was about to get schooled. I know my son, and the wheels were turning.

He turned the paper to face me. At the top, in his handwriting, it read, ALL THINGS DAD CAN DO WITH A BUM KNEE. The paper was now supported on his iPad, and a pen was in his hand, like a big business transaction was about to go down. "Let's list all the things you can do. I'll help you get started."

Can you fish? *Yes.*

Can you do dentistry? *Yes.*

Can you still fly your airplane? Something I had learned to do seven years earlier. *Yes.*

Can you still lecture? *Yes.*

Can you swim? *Yes.*

Can you ride a bike? *Yes.*

Can you still go on vacation? *Yes.*

Can you go to the movies? *Yes.*

Can you go out to dinner? *Yes.*

Can you watch Lifetime?

Okay, that part was a bit embarrassing. I hesitated. I looked at Cornell, who was on the verge of cracking up. That question was a dig, but *yes*. And more questions, and more *yeses*.

Cornell sat up and looked me dead in the eyes. "Dad, can you be happy with a bum knee?"

I didn't need to think about it. "Yep." I smiled, and reached over and gave him a big hug. I had learned my lesson. Again! Thick, I may be, but sooner or later, with Cornell's help, I get it.

"Great." And he jumped to his feet and was gone.

It became crystal clear to me, on that beautiful morning, how Cornell has not only survived, but thrived with all of his challenges. He's the poster child for *the glass is half full* mentality. Cornell refuses to look at what he cannot do and only focuses on what he can.

Thinking back to that conversation, there must have been a part of him that thought, *You are pouting about a sore knee? Are you kidding me?* He probably wanted to put a big *Phat L* on my forehead and laugh at me!

He didn't do that. The little baby who would never walk, talk, or be able to express his love, took the time to reframe a negative scenario in my head, even when he knew it wasn't all that tragic. He nicely taught me, "Dad, you still have so much to be thankful for. Let's focus on that."

—∞—

Cornell is grateful in all things: his life, his gifts, and the obstacles that test him. In a strange way, he seems to embrace the challenges as his greatest gifts of all. He's reached a deep understanding that without adversity, there can be no happiness. He has embraced the mysterious yin and yang of life. And he has taught it to me, student to teacher.

Kim and I have often been complimented for Cornell's demeanor and attitude, as though, somehow, we raised him to have this outlook on life. Make no mistake: this was hardwired into him. We have certainly provided him opportunities to grow, but his outlook on life comes from him. What I have learned is that these amazing traits can rub off onto other people. They can have a profound effect on those around him who are smart enough to pay attention. The reality is, his impact on our lives, and what we have all accomplished and created because of our exposure to this amazing person, far surpasses the impact we have had on his.

But I think it is best to let my daughter, Kaitlyn, have the final word about her brother Cornell:

> I was thinking about society's view of success and intelligence and how Cornell would fit into that box. As a child, I never saw the extent of his disabilities. Regardless of how many times my parents would talk to me about the extent of his knowledge, or the kind of jobs he could maybe get, or their concerns if he would ever get married, I always just kind of brushed it off.
>
> To me he was always normal, growing up with him was the only thing I had ever known. I had always thought that growing up with him made me softer, less likely to judge the world around me. To some extent that is true. I really don't see race, or any of the stereotypes that seem to go with it these days.
>
> One day I was in Walmart and I was annoyed that the cashier was taking a really long time to check people out. I started wondering why he was being so lazy. As I got closer to the counter I realized he probably had some sort of disability, and guilt hit me like a ton of bricks. This interaction happened when I was a senior in high school, when we were still very unsure of what type of job Cornell would be able to take. It was during a time where sometimes I would listen in on my parent's conversations, or catch them looking at Cornell, and I could just kind of see the worry in their stares.
>
> As I was standing there in that Walmart line, I realized that working a cashier line at Walmart would be very hard for him.

He had always struggled with money and counting, so being able to count money and deal with that at a register would be an amazing job for him to be able to retain, and more important than that, he would be both extremely happy and content with that job. I guess for the most part, it was just a realization that success should be measured by a person doing the most with what they can do.

If Cornell had ended up working at Walmart, no stranger passing by would look at him and think, "Wow, what ambition and persistence that young boy has, his life has become very successful." They would probably think more along the lines of, "He needs to get a real job." We live in a world that is incapable of seeing shades of gray, everything is either black and white, one thing or the other. A job at Walmart is not a "successful job" in our world. I know though, that success and knowledge should be measured on an individual basis, and Cornell is one of the most successful people I have ever met. Although he doesn't work at Walmart, his earning potential will be limited, and yet, he couldn't be happier. He has self-worth, he feels self- accomplishment, and he is living his life to the best of his abilities—mostly though, he is just happy. That is a successful life, and it is everything I strive to have in my life, as I am about to start the next chapter of my life and train for my career in dentistry.

I think the primary way Cornell changed me as a person, is that he was my drive and inspiration to work hard. I was upset and puzzled in high school when my friends, and especially my boyfriend at the time, often times were simply lazy; so much natural ability with academics and sports, and they would waste it. They wouldn't put in their best effort they wouldn't try their hardest. It was extremely frustrating for me to see that, and then to walk into my house to see my brother sitting at the kitchen table pulling at his hair, staring at a nickel and a dime, trying to figure out which one represents five cents. So that became my drive to get good grades. Those nights when I would come home exhausted, unmotivated to study, I would walk into the house and see him there, frustrated but still pushing through, and that would be my motivation. I would walk up the stairs and do my homework until I really felt ready. It is impossible for me to say if I would have ever gotten into dental school without him in my life. He made me appreciate being able to learn. He made me strive to be better.

Cornell is the epitome of grace. I've never seen a more forgiving or kind soul. Mean words never escape his mouth, he rarely shows any displays of anger or frustration. He is so accepting of everything in life that comes his way. Simply put, I am a better person because of him.

My stepdad, H.D., stated it best when he said, "While we can't control what happens to us in life, we can control how we react." It is a beautiful thing when you embrace the incredible simplicity of the Cornell Effect that Kaitlyn and my entire family have known. *Have faith. Feel blessed. Nurture your gifts and cherish your obstacles. Don't hold bitterness in your heart; learn to forgive completely. Live your life grateful. Apply yourself 100 percent.*

And above all else, *choose*, to love your life.

EPILOGUE

In summer of 2017, I was a little worried about Cornell. Kaitlyn had graduated from Virginia Tech and had moved on to the University of Louisville School of Dentistry. Kristen was in her second year at Virginia Tech, had a new boyfriend, and was thriving. Cornell was working at Interchrome Dental Lab and doing fine. But occasionally, I sensed that he missed having the full college experience.

Since Kaitlyn entered the university in 2012, we had become die-hard Hokie fans. Kaitlyn was the first to go all in. Cornell and I were second. Kim and Kristen initially came for the tailgating and the social aspects, but soon learned the game and were screaming at the top of their lungs like the rest of us. I bought season tickets, and nearly every home game, we found ourselves making the five-hour trip to Blacksburg.

Quite simply, we loved everything about it. We loved seeing our girls, we loved the quaint town of Blacksburg, we loved the tailgate experience, we loved the energy, and we loved the football.

So, during the summer of 2017, in search of finding a way to get Cornell closer to the university experience, I found myself writing a letter to the head football coach, Justin Fuente. In a page and a half, I described Cornell's situation, his attitude on life, and my hope that attending a practice, and meeting him and some of the team, could have a positive effect and make Cornell feel closer to the university he loves. I concluded the letter by saying that I realized it was a very big ask, and I would understand if it was not possible. I sent the letter out on a Wednesday morning, really not expecting to hear anything back.

On Saturday, I worked in the yard for a while, and when I got back to my phone, there was a voicemail from the Blacksburg area. My girls were both home so I thought for a second who it might be from.

"No, it couldn't be," I said to myself. I hit play.

"Hello, John, this is Coach Justin Fuente. I just came off the practice field and got your letter. Obviously, an amazing story, about Cornell. We want to do anything that we can to help. If that involves a practice, or getting on the field before a game, we are open to all of that." And then he proceeded to give me the phone number to his director of operations, whom we could call to set something up.

Needless to say, I sat there, completely astonished. Kim came around the corner, took one look at me, and said, "What's wrong?"

"You are not going to believe this. Cornell, come here, buddy!"

Calls were made, and we got invited to attend a practice following the Duke game toward the end of the coming season. I had Cornell listen to the voicemail and put the date on his calendar. Needless to say, we were all excited.

What I love the most about Virginia Tech football is that it's a good program, but not yet an elite program. I know, as a fan, that may sound crazy, because we all want to win. But I have come to love to watch the struggle. I love watching kids like Greg Stroman, a two-star athlete coming out of high school, struggle his first couple of years, only to become a dominant defensive back in the Atlantic Coast Conference, and one of the best punt returners in school history. Greg got drafted and is currently with the Washington Football Team in the NFL.

I think about the Edmunds brothers: Trey, Tremaine, and Terrell, all three-star athletes out of Danville, Virginia. These guys were legendary in their attitude and work ethic. Terrell and Tremaine would end up being drafted in the first round of the 2018 NFL draft (the first siblings to be drafted in the first round of the same draft, ever). Today all three brothers are on rosters in the NFL.

Then there are guys like Sam Rogers. Sam was a fullback who passed up scholarship offers at non–Power Five schools to walk on for the Hokies. He became one of the most dominant leaders on the team, scoring multiple times, most notably in the epic win against Ohio State, in the shoe. He had a short flirtation at the next level and is now following his coaching dreams at the high school level.

I simply love watching the kids grow.

So, I was more than excited to be able to peek behind the veil of our beloved Hokies. I was also excited to see Cornell's reaction to the players, and maybe the players' reactions to him.

The 2017 Duke game was a monsoon. And the Hokies, thankfully, decisively beat the Blue Devils. So, as we entered the facility on that Sunday evening, we were hoping all would be in good spirits.

After a detailed tour of the locker rooms, medical/training facilities, and lecture halls, we got to take the walk that the players make every game day. From the locker room, around the outdoor practice field, through the tunnel, and into Lane stadium. I could almost feel the building shake as the 65,000 fans jumped to "Enter Sandman." It was totally cool.

Then we were led to the indoor facility, where practice was in progress. Coach Fuente immediately came over to us, shook hands, welcomed us, and then addressed Cornell. "So, young man, it was raining really hard yesterday. Did you stay the *whole* game"?

"Yes, I did!" he responded with a big smile.

"Amazing. If I was in the stands, I am not sure I would have made it. What was it about the game that made you stay?"

"Well, I kind of figured you might ask me, so I wasn't leaving."

With that Coach "Fu" had a big laugh, and they were buddies.

As practice ended, the players came over and met Cornell and signed the VT ball he'd brought with him. They posed for pictures, talked to him, and slapped him five. Almost to a T, they were respectful, engaging, polite, and wanting to make our visit memorable. Cornell was having a blast.

What I was taken aback by was the players. We see them with all the gear on, how hard they hit, and they look like warriors. With the helmets off, they were all kids, really. Young men with crystal-clear eyes, with a very defined purpose. They all came from different backgrounds, different races, different socio-economic conditions, all looking very much like a family passionately pursuing a common cause. Coach Fuente must have seen me staring.

He walked over to me and said, "It's amazing isn't it? They look so big and tough from the stands, but they are all students here at Virginia Tech. They have classes, many have girlfriends, some have family issues to contend with, and then they also have the responsibilities of a college athlete."

In that moment, I couldn't help but imagine what Cornell would give to have the opportunity these kids have. I thought about how far some of these kids would go if we could transplant Cornell's heart into their bodies. I wondered which one of them might be blessed with amazing talent, but had a chip on his shoulder about something— something that would ultimately get in the way of going all in. I also wondered which of them had the opposite circumstance—those who were not highly recruited players in high school, but who were applying some of the principles innate to Cornell and were rising to the top. I imagined how challenging it was for Coach Fuente to deal with all of that.

I sat there and marveled that the football team in front of me was a microcosm of the world we live in. We all have to come together and work toward a common cause. We all have to be responsible for our own actions and behaviors, to become the best we can be. Most importantly, to succeed, we all have to employ the best principles and strategies, to play the game.

When Kaitlyn was in high school, she wrote an essay about her brother. She did a deep dive, pondering the question I had wrestled with the majority of the time he has been with us. Why did God put Cornell on this Earth, at this time, with all his apparent challenges? Her conclusion was simple. *Cornell was put on this earth to inspire people.* He certainly has inspired us. I hope, after reading this, that he has the same *effect* on you.

ABOUT THE AUTHOR

Dr. John Cranham splits his time between Chesapeake and Smith Mountain Lake, Virginia. He shares his life with Kim of thirty years, and their three adult children, Cornell, Kaitlyn and Kristen. As a biracial family, and one that raised a child with special needs, they have faced many challenges that have bound them together. They believe the obstacles they have faced, have been their greatest blessings, and give them a unique view of the world.

John is an internationally respected dentist with expertise in cosmetic dentistry, implant dentistry, occlusal reconstruction, and TMJ/facial pain. Splitting his time between practice and teaching, he has become one of the most sought-after educators in dentistry; to date, he has presented over 1,500 full days of education all over the world.

While this is his first foray into publishing outside of his chosen profession, he has told Cornell's story from the podium hundreds of times. He often finishes his programs with a brief synopsis of what his family refers to as "the Cornell Effect." John feels strongly that of all the things he teaches, this has the greatest impact. He hopes it has a similar effect on those of you who read it.

CPSIA information can be obtained
at www.ICGtesting.com
Printed in the USA
LVHW111259270422
717371LV00012B/131

9 781647 042646